CW00530473

Advance Praise fo

"*Ultra-Something* is easily the most cor   k
on running I have ever read. Brendan br........ .. ..il-
ity. And those of us who run are constantly humbled by this sport. While running
gives us big dreams, it also shows us the naked likelihood of never achieving them.
Brendan reminds us that having lofty goals is fun and necessary, but that the real
victory is simply lacing up the shoes and getting out the door."
—Sanjay Rawal, director, *3100 Run and Become, Gather, Food Chains*

"Winning despite the fact that he's (never) winning, Brendan Leonard is refresh-
ingly irreverent, emotionally honest, searingly wise, and, always, highly motivated
by pizza. This book may not turn you into a nature-loving ultra runner, but it
will certainly help you understand how doing very hard things can make us better
humans."
—Florence Williams, author of *The Nature Fix: Why Nature Makes us Happier,
Healthier, and More Creative*

"'Why would you do something like that?' is a question every ultrarunner has
received—usually from a wide-eyed, slack-jawed acquaintance who seems equal-
ly concerned and confused by the idea of running 100 miles. In *Ultra-Something*, Brendan Leonard answers that (perfectly reasonable) question, offering
a poignant, insightful, at times hilarious examination of his unlikely journey in
ultra-endurance sports. Whether you're a Hardrock 100 finisher or just signed up
for your first 50K, you'll glean valuable wisdom and inspiration from Leonard's
deep dive into the 'why' of ultrarunning."
—Ed Roberson, Creator and Host, Mountain & Prairie

"Writing about running can feel a lot like trying to describe a dream. What
feels urgent and personal to one can feel (at best) cliche or abstract to others.
Ultra-Something manages to distill the weird and wiggly parts of ultrarunning
into a genuinely fun and relatable read. Brendan has long been a sort of poet
laureate for the mid-pack runner, turning hilarious musings about what brings
us to this truly goofy sport into reflections on what it means to be human. This
trail-running memoir stands apart in the running space for its humor, humanity,
and true appreciation for the French fry. As an ultrarunner, I often get asked
about what I think about when I run. The answer for me, right now, is this book.
And also French fries."
—Zoë Rom, Editor-in-Chief, *Trail Runner/Outside Run*,
host and producer, The Outside Show

"Part ethnography, part memoir, and part ode, *Ultra-Something* lays bare all the absurdities and euphorias of ultrarunning. This is Brendan Leonard at his best, full of his trademark enthusiasm, humility, and wit—asking if maybe we don't just want to join him on a run. I loved it."
—Eliot Treichel, author of *A Series of Small Maneuvers* and *Close Is Fine*

"In *Ultra-Something*, Brendan Leonard offers us a gift, a deeply personal kaleidoscopic view into how humans create meaning and connection in the most arbitrary ways, not only through hero's journey revelation but in the prosaic edge zones of our own manufactured discomfort. Traversing pop culture, scientific studies, and memoir, Leonard leads us through an entertaining—often surprising—Rat Park of stories about how humans engineer self-worth out of thin air. The deeper you trust Leonard's masterful coin-collector mind, the clearer the picture becomes of his commitment to locating hope through endurance, that one of our greatest superpowers as humans is that we continually attempt to find ourselves through stubborn engagement with curiosity. This wide-reaching book is a constellation of anecdote and history that will make you laugh, then feel, then go forth into a world infinite in its possibilities of connection."
—Nicholas Triolo, Editor, *Trail Runner/Outside Run*

"Lab mice that run ultras. The quirky pain science of masochists. Trailside hallucinations. Brendan Leonard alternates ultra tales from around the world with his own long-day-and-night-out moments that will have you spitting electrolyte through your nostrils. When you're done with this ultramarathon of laughs and Leonard's wonderful illustrations, put it spine-out to impress family and friends."
—*Doug Mayer, author of* The Race that Changed Running: The Inside Story of UTMB

"I don't know how to describe *Ultra-Something* other than to say it's the most Brendan Leonard thing I've ever read: odd and a little all over the place but creatively told, relatable, and funny as hell. It's really ... something!"
—Mario Fraioli, Creator and Host, The Morning Shakeout

"Brendan Leonard understands the value in the tedious and the everyday. All of those little, un-sexy, sometimes annoying tasks and obligations that, in aggregate, compose an attentive life. And if we're not paying attention—to how we treat others, to how we treat ourselves—what's even the point?"
—Anton Krupicka, 2-time winner, Leadville Trail 100

ULTRA-SOME THING

BRENDAN LEONARD

WITH ILLUSTRATIONS BY THE AUTHOR

Copyright © 2024 by Brendan Leonard

All rights reserved.

ISBN: 979-8-9902273-9-2

No portion of this book may be reproduced in any form without written permission from the publisher or author, except as permitted by U.S. copyright law.

Ultra-Something

Prologue

At the finish line of the 2015 Western States Endurance Run, arguably the most famous and most prestigious American ultramarathon, the crowd suddenly became energized. A runner was coming, entering the Placer High School track, where the 100-mile race ends after winding up and over California's Sierra Nevada mountains from Olympic Valley Ski Resort.

Spectators cheered, clapped, and frantically rang cowbells, as the runner, Gunhild Swanson, rounded the track. A group of runners who had joined her peeled off at the start of the straightaway, clearing the way for her finish. The sides of the track were lined with people anxiously yelling "Come on, come on!" and other words of encouragement which sounded more like worried hope. More spectators ran across the infield, and a few paralleled her on the other side of the barrier fence set up on the track. Dozens of cameras and phones recorded her as she chugged toward the white finish arch, her strides shortened by 99-plus miles of mountain running and hiking over the previous day and a half. As she crossed the timing mat at the finish, the crowd erupted, hundreds of arms popping up into the air in a coordinated burst of emotion. Three feet past the finish line, the runner bent at the waist, hands on her knees, exhausted but grateful to be finished. Online videos of this minute of running would be watched hundreds of thousands of times[1].

Gunhild Swanson had finished dead last, 254th out of 254 runners. When she crossed the finish line on the track, the clock above her head read:

She had beaten the final 30-hour cutoff time by six seconds.

When that year's winners, Rob Krar and Magdalena Boulet, crossed the same finish line hours earlier, in 14:48:59 and 19:05:21, respectively, the scene was almost serene in comparison: some applause, some cheering, but with the overall energy and volume turned down.

The climax of Sylvester Stallone's 1976 movie *Rocky*, when boxer Rocky Balboa finally squares off with the defending champion, Apollo Creed, only lasts about nine minutes, but might be the most famous boxing match in film history.

Apollo, who had been scheduled to defend his title against a boxer who was injured, needs to find a new opponent, and decides to put on a show: As the original fight was scheduled to take place during America's bicentennial year in 1976 in Philadelphia, Apollo says he'll fight an up-and-coming boxer. Rocky Balboa, a Philly club fighter with more heart than skill, is chosen.

When the fight begins, everyone, including Rocky and Apollo, is surprised that Rocky actually lasts more than a few rounds, even landing some good punches, and as the fight drags on, ends up making it longer in the ring than any other boxer has against Apollo.

After Apollo knocks Rocky down during the 14th round and he battles to pull himself back up, the camera cuts to two people who we believe have much better judgment as far as Rocky's well-being: First, the trainer, Mick, who growls from just outside the ropes to Rocky, "Down. Stay down." Then, Rocky's girlfriend Adrian, who has just entered the arena to see Rocky at his worst, writhing in pain on the canvas. She looks away.

Rocky staggers in his corner like a drunken man trying to get back up on a barstool. Apollo stands in his corner with both arms raised. Rocky gets up at the count of nine. Apollo drops his arms and his jaw in disbelief. Just before the bell, Rocky lands a shot to Apollo's ribs.

When both fighters are in their corners, Apollo's trainer says to him, "You're bleeding inside, Champ. I'm gonna stop the fight."

Apollo replies, "You ain't stopping nothing, man."

Rocky's team cuts the swollen skin around his eye so he can see again, and Rocky stands up, saying to Mick, "You stop this fight, I'll kill you."

The two haggard fighters trade punches throughout the 15th and final round, mumbling promises to each other that there will be no re-match, and the bell rings, both men barely upright, but having survived. A bloodied Rocky calls out for Adrian, who finds her way to the ring, where she and Rocky profess their love for each other.

In the 1979 book, *Screenplay: The Foundations of Screenwriting*, Syd Field laid out what would come to be known as "Field's Paradigm," or the Three-Act Structure. Every screenplay, or actually, the story that forms a screenplay, Field argued, has three acts: set-up, confrontation, and resolution. The three-act structure is often drawn as a diagram, in various levels of complexity. A simple version might look like this:

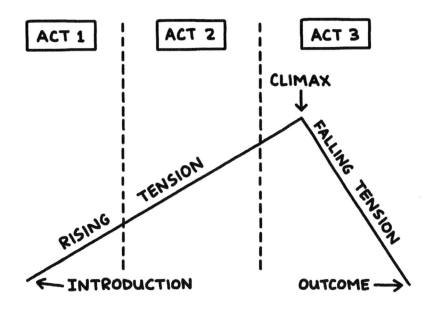

Rocky went on to be a surprise box office success, and was nominated for nine Academy Awards, winning three, including Best Picture. The film spawned eight sequels over the next four and a half decades.

One scene in the original film, in which Rocky goes on a training run and ends by sprinting up the steps at the Philadelphia Museum of Art, became famous, inspiring tourists to run up the stairs, and prompting tributes and parodies of the scene in other films and TV shows. The 72 steps themselves became known colloquially as the "Rocky Steps," and before the premiere of *Rocky III*, Stallone commissioned an eight-and-a-half-foot statue of Rocky to be built and placed at the top of the steps. Philadelphia City Commerce Director Dick Doran welcomed the statue and said Stallone had done more for Philadelphia's image "than anyone since Ben Franklin."

Rocky Balboa did not win the fight in *Rocky*. As the closing theme music builds, the ring announcer calls the fight "the greatest exhibition of guts and stamina in the history of the ring," and then announces the split decision in favor of Apollo Creed.

The plot of *Rocky*, as well as the plots of all eight sequels, per the three-act structure, might look like this:

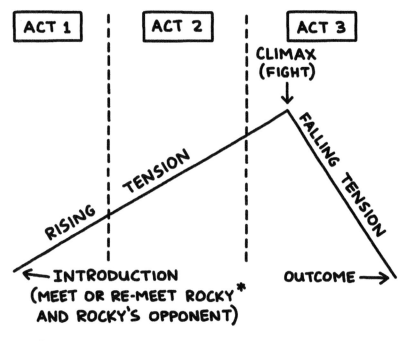

ACT 1   ACT 2   ACT 3

CLIMAX (FIGHT)

RISING TENSION

FALLING TENSION

←— INTRODUCTION
(MEET OR RE-MEET ROCKY*
AND ROCKY'S OPPONENT)

OUTCOME —→

*ADONIS CREED IN LATER SEQUELS

At almost any marathon race in the United States, there is a solid chance you will hear, played on a sound system near the starting line, or on a spectator's stereo along the race route, one of two songs, if not both: The song "Gonna Fly Now," also known as "Theme from *Rocky*" (a version of which appears in the first five *Rocky* movies), and the Survivor song "Eye of the Tiger," commissioned by Sylvester Stallone for *Rocky III*.

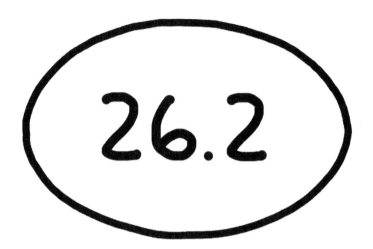

Every year around the world, about 1.1 million people run a marathon, an organized race that's 26.2 miles, or 42.195 kilometers. The story of why we do this dates back to 490 BC: During the first Persian invasion of Greece, a heavily outmanned Athenian army defeated the Persian forces in battle near the town of Marathon, Greece. A herald named Pheidippides was chosen to deliver the news of the victory to Athens. He ran the entire distance of 26.2 miles/42.195 kilometers, addressed the magistrates in session saying something like, "Joy to you, we've won!" and then died on the spot.

The Greeks also created the tradition of the Olympic Games, held every four years, or each Olympiad, from 776 BC to 393 AD. The ancient Olympic Games never had a marathon race—the "long-distance race," or dolichos, introduced in the 15th Olympiad, was somewhere between four and nine kilometers (approximately 2.5 to 5.5 miles). The last recorded ancient Olympic Games were held in 393 A.D., after which they took a 1500-year hiatus.

When the Olympic Games were revived in 1896 in Athens, the first marathon race was held, celebrating Pheidippides' legendary (and fatal) run from Marathon to Athens. A few months later, the Knickerbocker Athletic Club organized a marathon race from Stamford, Connecticut to The Bronx, and in March 1897, the Boston Athletic Association held the first-ever Boston Marathon. From there, the marathon race spread all over the world.

If you signed up to participate in a running race, such as a marathon or a 10K, your personal journey could also be seen as three acts:

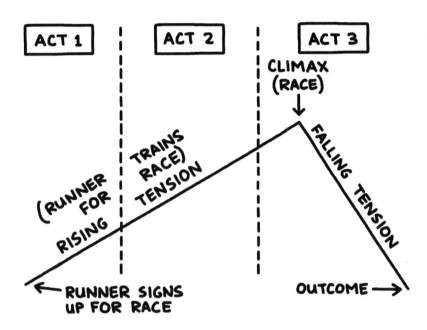

No one, from the fast runners hoping to win the race to the people just hoping to finish, has any idea how their race is going to go. As the race day draws near, tension builds, whether you feel it or not, and the only thing that releases all that tension is the actual running of the race. When it's over, whether you're happy with the result or not, it's over.

The first time Ray Yoder ate at a Cracker Barrel, he wasn't that impressed. He was in Nashville in 1978, helping to set up an RV show at the Opryland Resort and Convention Center, and there was a Cracker Barrel nearby. So he ate there, and it didn't exactly blow his mind. But he had a job delivering RVs across the country from a manufacturer in his hometown of Goshen, Indiana, and he spent a lot of time on the road. So he found himself in a lot of places with Cracker Barrel restaurants. He kept eating at Cracker Barrels, and they started to grow on him.

He was almost always on the road by himself while his wife, Wilma, was at home raising their four children. When all the kids had finished school and moved out of their house, Wilma started to join Ray on the road. Around 1993, they realized they had eaten at lots of Cracker Barrel restaurants, and decided to try visiting all of them.

By August of 2017, the Yoders had both turned 81, and had visited almost all of the 600-plus Cracker Barrel restaurants in the United States, Ray mostly eating blueberry pancakes if it was breakfast time, meatloaf if he was there for lunch or dinner, and pot roast if it was Sunday. Cracker Barrel caught wind of Ray and Wilma's quest and flew them out to Portland to visit the newly-opened restaurant in Tualatin, Oregon, Number 645. A line of applauding Cracker Barrel employees greeted them at the door, with a bouquet of sunflowers and roses for Wilma, and custom aprons for both of them.

Their journey had taken them to 44 states, and Ray estimated they had driven more than 5 million miles. "Well, everybody does something, usually anyway," Ray said. "So we thought we would do this and it would be fun."

At the 2017 Run Rabbit Run starting line at the base of Colorado's Steamboat Ski Resort, 314 runners stood in the corral, every one of them hoping to finish the 102.5-mile race. Only about 58 percent of them would actually make it to the finish line.

The Run Rabbit Run is not typically mentioned as one of the hardest ultramarathon races in the United States, and 2017 wasn't an abnormally hot or difficult year. Generally, about one-third of people who start the race each year don't finish for one reason or another: injury, gastrointestinal distress, dehydration, exhaustion.

No one standing in that starting corral believed it was impossible for a human being to travel 102.5 miles of mountainous terrain in 36 hours. Everyone was aware that it was something humans did. They had heard of these types of races before, maybe knew someone who had completed one, or maybe they'd even run this one in a previous year and had fun doing it. They believed they could be one of the people who earned a Run Rabbit Run 100 finisher belt buckle, and that's why they were standing just inside the red start/finish arch, pacing, chatting with other runners, shaking out their nervous legs.

I was there too, standing in the corral, anxious and jittery, with a race number pinned to my running shorts, as the morning sun started to warm the high-altitude air. Like everyone else, I knew that people, arguably "normal" people who had day jobs and families and credit card bills, were perfectly capable of running a 100-mile mountain ultramarathon in 36 hours. It was something that had been done plenty of times before by human beings just like me.

Well, maybe not like me. I wasn't sure if I'd be just like them, a finisher. And I'd been unsure for eight months, since I'd paid my entry fee.

I was still unsure when the gun went off and the crowd of runners started shuffling forward through the starting arch. I started jogging with them, and no one tried to stop me, so I just kept going.

My first long-distance run, when I was eight years old, took this route: Out the front door of our house at 1308 Cherry Street in Red Oak, Iowa, down Crestline Avenue past the house of my classmate Jana Podliska, past Ed Collins' house (whose driveway basketball hoop had a net that had become petrified over years of disuse, which I'd discovered when my basketball got stuck in it), right on Birch Street for a half-block, left on Eastern Avenue, past the first rental house we lived in when we moved to town and the site of my first musical memory (my dad listening to cassette copies of *Abbey Road* on Sundays), out to Highway 34, where I turned around to go back the way I came. By the time I hit Crestline Avenue on my return trip, running in a pair of L.A. Gear high-tops, my legs and lungs burned. It was all I could do to hang on and try to keep up some speed until I hit the finish line, our driveway, where I bent over, hands on knees, and tried to catch my breath. It was a run I'd do again and again.

This route was exactly one mile, clocked by my mom using the odometer in her blue 1983 Pontiac Grand Prix. My mom was a runner, the first adult I'd ever known who ran for fun. She ran five miles a day, five days a week, for 10 years in her 30s and early 40s. She ran 5K and 10K races, and would usually place second or first in her age group, depending on if Paula Odefey was running the race or not.

I first ran the mile from our house and back either because I had told my mom I was bored, or because the Presidential Physical Fitness test was coming up in my sixth-grade gym class: we'd run four laps around our crushed-cinder high school track, with our gym teacher clocking us on his stopwatch. I had no idea what a "fast" mile was, but a couple guys in my brother's class, a year ahead, had broken seven minutes. I hoped to get something under eight minutes.

I had no idea how to pace myself, how fast to try to run the first lap, how to conserve energy for the last lap, or that running shoes existed in my size (although in the next year, my shoe size would overlap with my mom's for a few months, and I'd wear her hand-me down Asics for a while). All I knew was that seven and a half minutes or eight minutes was an incredibly long time for someone to keep running nonstop.

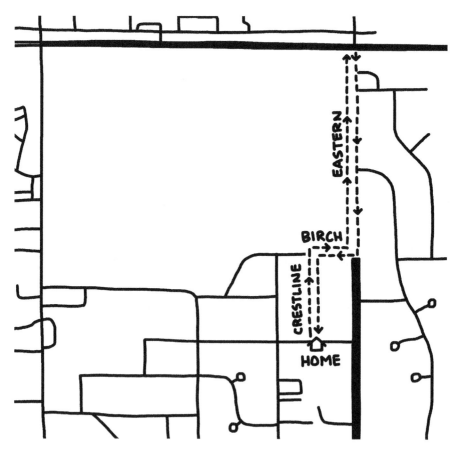

Ultrarunning, by definition, is the act of participating in a footrace longer than 26.2 miles or 42.195 kilometers.

Most ultramarathons, though, come in sizes of 31 miles/50 kilometers, 50 miles/80.5 kilometers, 62 miles/100 kilometers, and 100 miles/161 kilometers. Designing a 26.3-mile/42.3-kilometer "ultramarathon" would be a bit like a fast-food restaurant adding a single French fry to a "medium" size and calling it a "large" order.

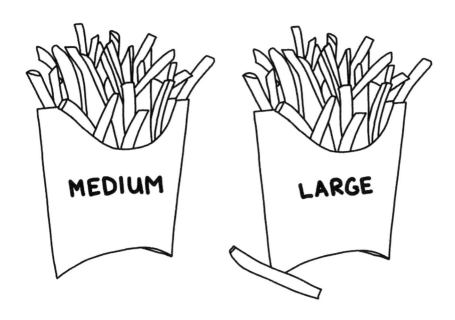

Page 106, *Relentless Forward Progress: A Guide to Running Ultramarathons*, by Bryon Powell[2]:

Walking, Your New Best Friend

Think Walking is anathema to trail running? You're wrong. It's all a matter of degrees. Even the world's best trail runners walk when the terrain, slope, and distance dictate that they do so.

Before figuring out when you should walk while trail running, you must first decide that you are willing to walk. This might be more difficult for runners who have primarily run shorter distances or who have come from a road running background. Know that you're not swallowing your pride when you walk. You're simply taking part in an activity that includes both running and walking.

You might ask, "Well, isn't it disingenuous to call it 'ultrarunning,' then?" Maybe it is.

People all around the world who watch football probably have the same question about the American sport called "football," a game in which the players move the ball about 90 percent of the time using their hands, not their feet.

"Some people in the distance-running community derisively refer to ultrarunners as 'hobby joggers' or 'glorified fast-walkers.'"

—Joseph Bien-Kahn, *The New York Times Magazine*, Feb. 11, 2020

"Ultras are just eating and drinking contests, with a little exercise and scenery thrown in."

—Sunny Blende, ultramarathon nutritionist, *Born to Run: A Hidden Tribe, Superathletes, and the Greatest Race the World Has Never Seen*

ONE FREE PERSONAL
PAN PIZZA FOR EACH
STAR STICKER

Pizza Hut began its BOOK IT! literacy program in 1984, at the direction of Pizza Hut's president, Arthur Gunther, whose son had difficulty learning to read when he was growing up. Kids who participated in the program would receive a certificate for one free one-topping personal pan pizza after reading a required number of books. Each month, a student could earn one pizza, and the program went on for five months of the school year.

During my third-grade year of elementary school in 1987-88, I read dozens of books, even after I'd earned my free pizza for the month. I began to skip going outside for recess to stay inside and read, sitting alone at my desk in Mrs. Martinez's classroom. After a while, Mrs. Martinez started to worry about me, and mentioned to my mom that maybe I should go outside during recess a few times a week? So I did, semi-reluctantly. I played football with a group of boys, catching the occasional pass. But I kept reading in my spare time, cranking out book reports for extra credit, and beyond, even when there was no academic incentive. Playing football on the playground was fun, especially if Mark Roberts saw that I was open and fired a pass my way, and I managed to catch it without it bouncing off my chest. But I couldn't wait to get back to whatever book I was tearing through that week.

One of my favorite books in third grade was Robert C. O'Brien's *Mrs. Frisby and the Rats of NIMH*, a Newbery Medal-winning story about a widowed field mouse, Mrs. Frisby, who has a sick child and must move her house and family before it gets plowed over by a farmer. She enlists the help of mysterious rats who live across the farm from her—who, as she finds out, were lab rats who underwent a series of experiments at the National Institute of Mental Health. The rats learned to read and wire electricity into their nests. And because of steroid injections, they didn't age. Nicodemus, the rats' leader, explains their backstory to Mrs. Frisby for the middle third of the book:

I had been in what is called a maze, a device to test intelligence and memory. I was put in it many times again, and so were the others. The second time I got through it a little faster, because I remembered—to some extent—which corridors had electric floors and which did not. The third time I was still faster; and after each trial George (or sometimes Julie, sometimes Dr. Schultz) would write down how long it took. You might ask: Why would I bother to run through it at all, if I knew it was only a trick? The answer is I couldn't help it. When you've lived in a cage, you can't bear <u>not</u> to run, even if what you're running toward is an illusion.

In 1987, either my brother or I picked up the trade paperback edition of the *Guinness Book of World Records* at the school book fair. I spent a lot of time with that book, not reading it cover-to-cover, but flipping open to a page and marveling at the shortest, longest, smallest, largest, heaviest, and fastest things recorded by humans. The black-and-white image of Shridhar Chillal, the Indian man who dedicated his life to growing the world's longest fingernails (and also, somehow, photography), was burned into my brain. He held his left hand out to the side, showing his 2-foot-long winding fingernails and his circular thumbnail. Even now, three decades later, I could probably draw the image from memory.

The book was partly a testament to athletic achievement, but I loved the people who figured out some weird thing they liked and went after it with a passion so intense that they ended up getting their name in the world record books: The woman who managed to peel one continuous 172-foot apple skin in Rochester, New York, in 1976. The guy who threw a single playing card 185 feet in Dearborn, Michigan, in 1979. The guy who made 5,247 omelets in 36 hours in Providence, Rhode Island, in 1985.

I couldn't believe the human endurance feats, until I flipped to page 436 one day and read through the text under the "Balancing on One Foot" world record: "The longest recorded duration for balancing on one foot is 34 hours by Shri N. Ravi in Sathy Amangalam City, Tamil Nadu, India, April 17-18, 1982. The disengaged foot may not be rested on the standing foot nor may any sticks be used for support or balance, *but 5-minute rest breaks are allowed after each hour.*"

So many world records seemed superhuman, but many of them had rules like this, permitting breaks or other allowances. It was a small revelation—maybe some of the world record holders weren't superhuman, but ... regular humans who were extremely motivated?

I was nervous the day we were scheduled to run the mile in my seventh grade P.E. class, unable to eat much of my lunch in fear that it would give me a cramp, or I'd vomit it all up. It wasn't fair, I thought, that some kids would get to run the mile in the morning, after eating whatever they wanted at home, not Salisbury steak or turkey tetrazzini or whatever I'd be eating off a melamine compartment plate less than an hour before. After lunch, we'd hop on a school bus to ride out to the Red Oak High School track, a non-state-of-the-art crushed cinder surface surrounding the football field where our varsity team would win either one game, or zero games, every fall.

I had sort of timed myself running down the block from our house to the highway and back, one mile according to my mom's car. Timing myself using my blue calculator watch, I was able to get close to eight minutes. I felt like I was about to cough up blood as I tried to sprint with lead in my legs down the final straightaway to the house.

My class spread out on the track, filling what would have been all eight lanes, if they were marked. At the whistle, we took off, and I went out too fast. I also knew I was going too fast, but I hoped the adrenaline of the day would carry me. I kept thinking "pace yourself," and not pacing myself, and by lap two I was feeling it—my pace was unsustainable. I slowed down because I had no choice, and the anxiety of possibly blowing it crept up my stomach. Other kids were already walking, but I couldn't allow myself. Lap three was even slower, and the finish line seemed impossibly far away as my legs and arms burned. A light rain started as I rounded the first curve, and I knew I'd done everything wrong and was paying for it.

I coasted in on fumes, my feet slamming into the cinder every step. Mr. Tidgren called out my time as I crossed the finish line: seven fifty-something. As I put my hands behind my head and walked down the straightaway to try to catch my breath, I knew one thing: when track season came around, I would try anything besides the mile.

We split into two lines, every one of us drenched in sweat under our clunky pads and helmets. The weather during football two-a-day practices had to be the hottest two weeks of every Iowa summer, and with the humidity on top of it, you were drenched the second you walked out of the house in shorts and a T-shirt, let alone a plastic helmet with an inch and a half of padding, plus shoulder pads and knee-length pants with pads sticking to your hips, thighs, and kneecaps. By my junior year, I was used to it, having been through it twice already. But now it was time for the Okie Drill.

It was very uncomplicated: Two players lined up across from each other, both in three-point stances—both feet and one hand on the ground, knees bent, waiting to launch forward. When a coach blew the whistle, you'd explode forward out of your stance, into the other player, a few feet away. There wasn't a lot of strategy, just pure power. Stay low, keep your feet moving, and try to push the other player backward and/or down.

I was small for a football player, topping out at 156 pounds my senior season in high school, despite lifting weights as much as I could. My brother, one and a half years year older than me, was 175 pounds his senior year, and was, football-wise, a monster compared to me. He bench-pressed 315 pounds, started at guard on offense and linebacker on defense, and made the all-district team. We had moved to a different town, and Chad was happy to be on a team that could compete for the district title, and maybe even go to the state playoffs.

There were other sets of brothers on the team that year, and they faced off during the Okie Drill. The coaches set it up so I didn't have to get destroyed by my brother. It made sense, since we played different positions on both sides of the ball (or rather, he played, and I stood on the sidelines), but I think it was kind of an act of mercy, too. I went up against Brian Uglum, who was about the same size as me, but more athletic and aggressive. Brian definitely won our matchup, and both of us ended up on my side of the line, but it wasn't the absolute stomping I would have received from my brother.

The NFL banned the Oklahoma Drill in 2019, and the NCAA banned it in 2021.

At halftime of one of the pivotal games of my senior football season, we were surprised to find ourselves losing 14-0. In the shed under the bleachers, we all took a knee as our coaches tried to make sense of what had happened, and what we should do in the second half in order to win. One of our coaches was a screamer. He was a large man, who, at least once a game, would lay into a player on the sidelines, veins popping out of his neck and his face flushed red, yelling at a teenager loudly enough that the first few rows of people in the bleachers could make out what he was screaming.

For the first half of my senior year of high school I wholeheartedly believed that football was basically the quote, best days of my life, unquote, that we'd maybe go to state, and memories of that season would stay with me for decades. I tried hard. I wasn't that big, and I wasn't that fast, or explosive, so I wasn't in on that many plays that affected the outcome of the season. I caught a couple passes, usually for five or 10 yards, and one in the state playoff game. The coaches let me help pick the soundtrack for our highlight video at the end of the season, but I don't remember if I ever had the ball in my hands during any of the actual highlights. I liked a couple of my coaches, and did my best to not draw the attention of the third coach, the one who would often lose his temper and explosively berate a hunched-shouldered player on the sidelines.

During his halftime speech when we were down 14-0, he screamed at us for a couple minutes, his mouth a funnel for the rage erupting from deep recesses of his body. The shed was silent, with a murmur of spectators outside chattering as they lined up to get popcorn or soda before returning to their seats. I knelt on one knee pad, supporting myself with a hand holding the face mask of my helmet. Coach wound up and fired the apex of his soliloquy at all of us, at the highest volume he could muster: "Wipe the SHIT out of your PANTS and play some FOOTBALL."

Everyone knelt stone-faced, ashamed of our first-half effort. Exactly then, the absolute worst time it could have happened, the absurdity of the whole thing hit me, that we were just kids, that this game was only as important as we decided it was, that this wasn't the only thing I was going to do in my life, and that the world would keep spinning whether we won or lost. It was like I left my body and was seeing it from the outside for the first time ever. This was not war. This was comedy. I had no frame of reference for how our adult coach was acting, except for the Yosemite Sam cartoons I had watched on Saturday mornings as a young boy.

I closed my eyes and clenched my jaw, breathing slowly and deeply through my nose, hoping it looked like I was ingesting this halftime speech with the appropriate amount of seriousness. If I so much as giggled or half-snorted a few puffs of air through my nose to stifle a laugh, I might as well quit the team. I wasn't 100 percent sure that Coach wouldn't just grab my neck and throttle me in front of everyone, or throw me through a wall, leaving a football-player-shaped hole in the wood paneling. This was a serious situation—not the game, but the halftime speech. I exhaled and slowly pulled in one more breath through my nose.

We lost the game 21-7. Nobody died or anything. I did catch a pass in the second half.

Football is a complex game. You can spend hours and hours learning the ins and outs of its rules and strategies, and a lifetime learning its history, culture, and following the statistics, news, and narratives of each season. You can educate yourself by watching games, listening to sports talk radio or watching shows, understanding offensive and defensive strategies, to the point where you might even be able to predict a play or two before it happens on the TV in your living room: Watch this, they're going to go for it on fourth and three here.

But most football players stop playing football after 17 or 18. The supermajority of us are retired. Maybe you can play rec league flag football for a few years after high school, but the real game is out of almost everyone's reach beyond a certain age.

I spent hours of my teenage years studying plays, trying to get better, hoping for a few moments of success. The team arguably succeeded, making it to the state playoffs, so I was part of a big group of people working together to achieve a goal. But if I was really honest with myself, the team would not have suffered too much without my contributions had I decided to, say, run cross country or play in the marching band.

When our season ended my last year of high school and I got on with the rest of my life, all that effort only translated into one thing: being a football fan. But watching sports didn't really take for me. Given three hours on a Saturday or Sunday, and the choice between doing something myself and watching someone else do something on TV, I always chose doing something.

I woke up with a hangover at our college house in Cedar Falls, Iowa, one sunny summer weekday. I didn't have to work at my bartending job that night, so I had the whole day free. I had picked up a copy of Hunter S. Thompson's *Fear and Loathing in Las Vegas* and had yet to crack it open, but today was the day. Seemed like a nice day to sit on the stoop and read. I walked down to the convenience store a few blocks away and bought a watery coffee and a pack of Kamel Red Light cigarettes.

I had spent my first couple years of college gradually losing the fitness I'd acquired in high school. I had been almost religious with strength training in high school. I ran during other sports—pass patterns and sprints in football practice, up and down the court following the action and then in drills in basketball practice, all this with the metabolism and high hormonal output of a teenager.

I signed up for a rock climbing class my freshman year of college, missed the first class, took weight lifting instead, and made trips to the weight room a few times a week for a while, then got a job as a night janitor so I could earn some money, and then spent most of my nights off work partying, spending that money, and leaving no room for weight lifting. At the bar, I would have the occasional cigarette, telling myself that if I was going to be sitting in a room thick with all that secondhand smoke, I might as well get some firsthand. And then I started buying cigarettes, but only when I was out drinking. And then that one day before my junior year of college, I just thought it sounded nice to sit on the stoop, read, and smoke. There are 20 cigarettes in a pack, and each one of them took me almost exactly five minutes to smoke.

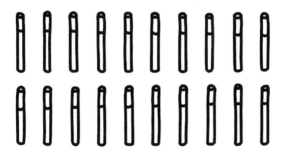

I finished the book, and the pack of cigarettes, in one day, and every day after that for a little more than six years, I smoked a pack of cigarettes. This was during the years when smoking indoors was gradually becoming illegal, so for the last half of that time, I had to go outside to smoke. If you do the math, I was spending over an hour and a half outside each day, inhaling and exhaling poisonous chemicals in order to access nicotine, which I was addicted to after the first pack of cigarettes.

The last two or three of those years, I wanted to quit smoking, because of all the reasons people usually want to quit smoking (early death, smells bad, expensive, et cetera), but just couldn't quite stop. I'd make it a day or two and then let myself off the hook and go buy a pack, and be right back in it for a few days or months, loving how it felt for the first minute or so of each cigarette, and then hating it and kind of hating myself too for the rest of the time.

By the time I quit, I would smoke around 42,000 cigarettes, which looks like this:

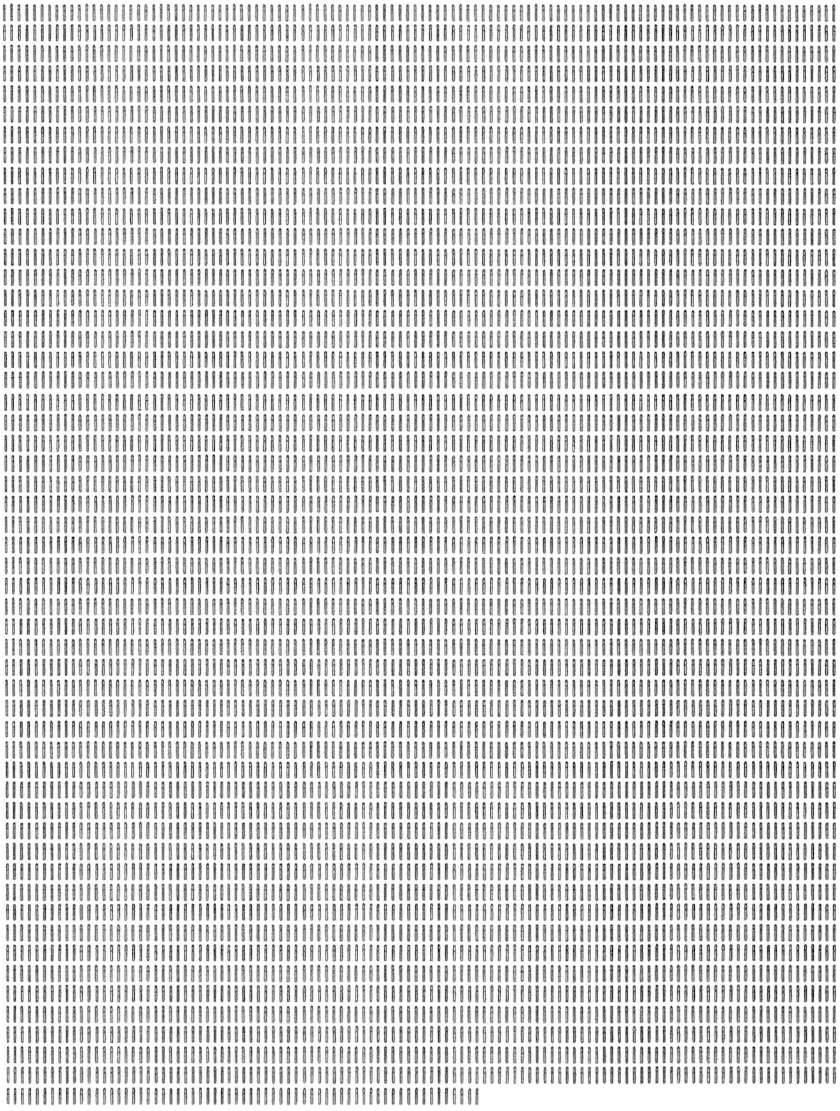

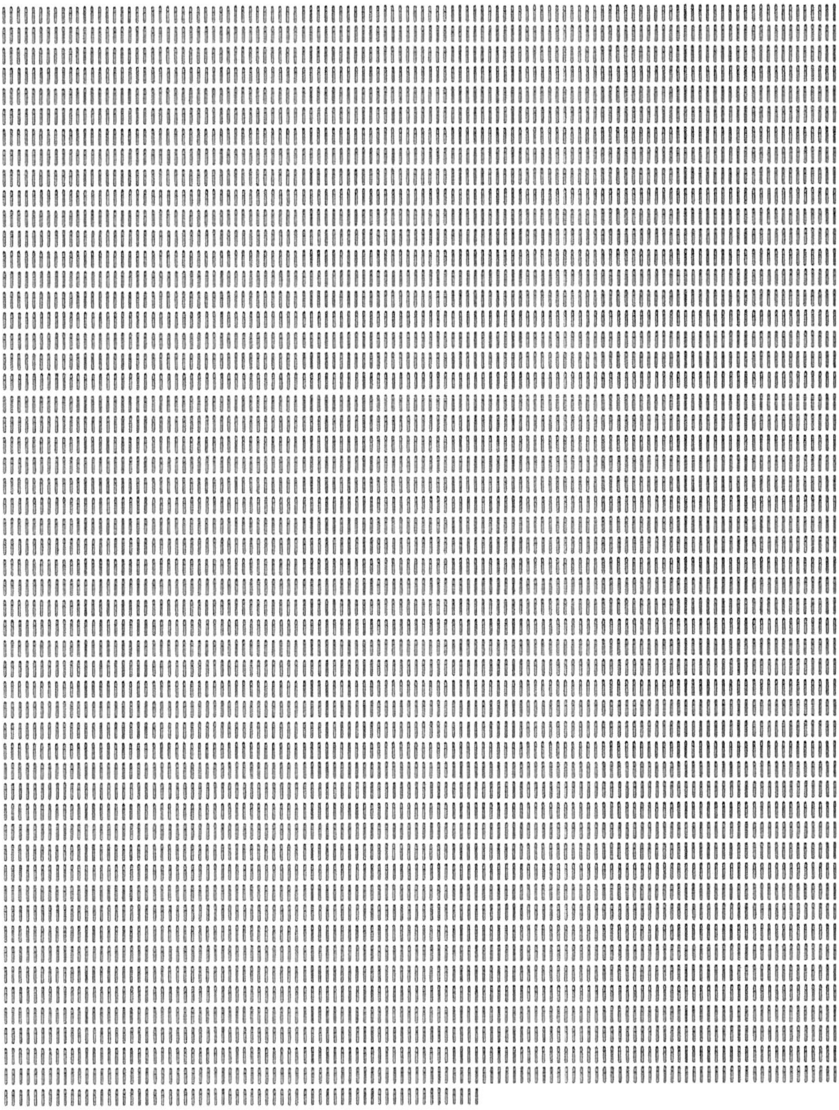

Which is about 3,500 hours of smoking, or almost 146 days straight, if you started at midnight on January 1.

		JAN				
S	M	T	W	T	F	S
					1	2
3	4	5	6	7	8	9
10	11	12	13	14	15	16
17	18	19	20	21	22	23
24	25	26	27	28	29	30
31						

		FEB				
S	M	T	W	T	F	S
	1	2	3	4	5	6
7	8	9	10	11	12	13
14	15	16	17	18	19	20
21	22	23	24	25	26	27
28						

		MAR				
S	M	T	W	T	F	S
	1	2	3	4	5	6
7	8	9	10	11	12	13
14	15	16	17	18	19	20
21	22	23	24	25	26	27
28	29	30	31			

		APR				
S	M	T	W	T	F	S
				1	2	3
4	5	6	7	8	9	10
11	12	13	14	15	16	17
18	19	20	21	22	23	24
25	26	27	28	29	30	

		MAY				
S	M	T	W	T	F	S
						1
2	3	4	5	6	7	8
9	10	11	12	13	14	15
16	17	18	19	20	21	22
23	24	25	26	27	28	29
30	31					

		JUNE				
S	M	T	W	T	F	S
		1	2	3	4	5
6	7	8	9	10	11	12
13	14	15	16	17	18	19
20	21	22	23	24	25	26
27	28	29	30			

		JULY				
S	M	T	W	T	F	S
				1	2	3
4	5	6	7	8	9	10
11	12	13	14	15	16	17
18	19	20	21	22	23	24
25	26	27	28	29	30	31

		AUG				
S	M	T	W	T	F	S
1	2	3	4	5	6	7
8	9	10	11	12	13	14
15	16	17	18	19	20	21
22	23	24	25	26	27	28
29	30	31				

		SEPT				
S	M	T	W	T	F	S
			1	2	3	4
5	6	7	8	9	10	11
12	13	14	15	16	17	18
19	20	21	22	23	24	25
26	27	28	29	30		

		OCT				
S	M	T	W	T	F	S
					1	2
3	4	5	6	7	8	9
10	11	12	13	14	15	16
17	18	19	20	21	22	23
24	25	26	27	28	29	30
31						

		NOV				
S	M	T	W	T	F	S
	1	2	3	4	5	6
7	8	9	10	11	12	13
14	15	16	17	18	19	20
21	22	23	24	25	26	27
28	29	30				

		DEC				
S	M	T	W	T	F	S
			1	2	3	4
5	6	7	8	9	10	11
12	13	14	15	16	17	18
19	20	21	22	23	24	25
26	27	28	29	30	31	

One Sunday bartending shift ended my career as a football fan. I showed up for work at 10 a.m., maybe a little hungover. My job was to open the bar, fill the ice buns, put back the floor mats, stock bottles, and most importantly, switch on all of the bar's 27 TVs. Once we opened, I made drinks, poured beer, washed bar glasses, hustled food, bussed tables. On Saturdays and Sundays during the fall, I was in charge of the TV remote controls. If a customer at a table wanted to watch the Bears game, I walked over and switched it. The bar sat 20 people along a U-shaped wooden counter, with me behind it, and eight TVs above my head.

Customers trickled in shortly after we opened the doors at 11 a.m., some there just for lunch and others, on the other end of the spectrum, wearing their favorite team's jerseys. On this Sunday, a few singles started sitting at the bar, ordering the occasional bloody Mary or beer, asking for a menu to order lunch now or a little later. The first round of games started at noon, and the next at 3 p.m.

A guy in his mid-50s sat down on a barstool on the left side of the bar and ordered a 22-ounce Miller Lite in a plastic souvenir cup. At $1.75 it was a steal, and also an opportunity for thrifty people to only tip the bartender a quarter. The guy asked me to put the Vikings game on one TV, and the Steelers game on another TV. The opening manager always made a cheat sheet of channels of all the days' games, so switching the TVs was no problem, aside from aiming the remote exactly at the right TV.

While the mechanics of changing channels were simple, the social order sometimes threw a wrench in things. Other customers might sit down and want to watch the Packers game, or the 49ers game. Thankfully, sports fandom is pretty much regional, so in Iowa, people mostly want to watch the Packers, Vikings, Bears, or Kansas City. But not always.

And of course, this Sunday was one of those times. We started to get busy, the bar filled up, the drink ticket printer spat out orders, my customers' food was up, and a keg blew, which meant at least two minutes of me wrestling the old one out and a new one into the cooler. And then someone else wanted to watch a different game over by the guy drinking a Miller Lite.

As I hustled to switch the kegs, a customer sitting a couple seats away from Miller Lite Man said Hey, could we get the 49ers game on this TV, and Miller Lite Man, who had drunk one-fourth of his beer in the hour he'd been sitting there, was not having it, believing the $1.75 he had spent made the four TVs closest to him part of his personal kingdom until 3 p.m.

I stood there, one ear listening to the printer buzz out more drink orders, the other ear listening to Miller Lite Man tell everyone that No, he was watching the Steelers game on this TV, the Vikings on that one, and the Eagles game (for some reason) on a third television. Someone at a table behind Miller Lite Man kindly requested that I leave the second TV from the right tuned to the Kansas City game, and that left the 49ers person out of luck. It was tense for a second, as Miller Lite Man sat with his arms crossed, shaking his head as if he were a bouncer guarding the door of a nightclub, listening to someone at the front of the line plead with him to please, please let them in even though the club was at capacity.

These people were not asking Miller Lite Man if they could come into his house and take a shit on his living room carpet; they just wanted to watch one football game compared to his three. Miller Lite Man, however, looked confident in the justness of his position—in his mind, he was clearly Jesus, this sports bar was his temple, and he was flipping the tables of the merchants and money changers.

Thankfully, one of the 49ers fans noticed that a table on the opposite side of the bar was open, and suggested to the other that they go sit over there. It was a little farther away from the TV, and it also meant I would lose two customers, and a tip from two customers, but at that point, I didn't care. They stood up, walked over to the host stand, and were escorted to a table. I switched out the keg, changed one of the TVs on the other side to the 49ers game, and started to catch up on making the printer drinks.

Miller Lite Man finished his beer three hours later, tipped me 25 cents, and no doubt eventually died without wondering if he had done the right thing that day at the sports bar. In the 20 years after I left that job, I never watched another football game.

One time, around 2005 or so, I remember reading a news story about cigarettes being as addictive as crack cocaine. That made me feel a lot better. I mean, I quit drinking, went to outpatient rehab for five weeks, and had made it three years into sobriety, but I thought quitting smoking was way harder. So I'd trot out that bit of info every once in a while to make myself feel better: "They're just as addictive as crack."

Then a few years later, I read a headline about another study: "Oreos as Addictive as Crack Cocaine."

Now, I am astonished when I meet someone who can limit themselves to the recommended serving size of just two Oreos, instead of an entire row of a package of them, like a normal person. But quitting Oreos, at least for me, is a walk in the park compared to quitting smoking.

My first apartment in Denver was on Gilpin Street, a little less than a block off Colfax Avenue.

A few hundred feet down the sidewalk to the north was a corner store where I bought my last pack of cigarettes ever, after six and a half years of smoking a pack a day. I had stopped smoking cold turkey for several weeks, but couldn't stop thinking about it, so I went down and bought a pack, smoked two of them, but didn't enjoy it as much as I thought I would. I left the other 18 cigarettes in the pack and stood it up in the middle of the sidewalk, where some lucky person would find it that night.

A few hundred feet up that same sidewalk to the south, across 14th Avenue and then 13th Avenue, was Cheesman Park, one of the most interesting parks in the city. At different points, it had been a cemetery for the indigent (most of whom had been dug up and relocated), and one of the busiest cruising spots in town for gay men (the Pride parade still starts there every year). A 1.7-mile crushed-rock path winds around the perimeter of the park, making it popular among walkers and runners. I had run a few laps around it over the course of my first summer and fall there, and decided it would be perfect for my final attempt at quitting smoking for good: training for, and running, a marathon.

I had a vague idea of how someone might train for a marathon, but didn't do much research. I knew you were supposed to gradually increase your longest run until you could run something around 20 miles, and that was about all I knew. I figured I'd run five miles (three laps around Cheesman Park) three times a week, and then on the weekend, I'd run a "long run." The training plan, if I stuck to it, would look like this:

And so on, until the biggest number was 20, or 21 or 22, a few weeks before the marathon.

My alarm would go off at 6 a.m., and I'd pull the covers down a couple inches, and the cold air in the bedroom would jab its fingers into any exposed skin. The bedroom in our apartment was a converted sun porch on the second floor, and you could literally see through gaps in the floorboards. I had bought a little space heater, but the bedroom was always cold.

I always took four or five minutes to collect my thoughts in the dark, hate myself, hate my stupid ideas, and slowly open my eyes, before reluctantly pulling the covers down and stepping out of bed with the quickness of ripping off a band-aid. I owned one pair of running pants, bought on sale as I was making $12.50 an hour at the newspaper and I hated running. I put them on, slid appropriate layers over my head and arms, grabbed some gloves and a hat, and trudged out the door. I gave myself a D- for Attitude, but a B+ for Discipline.

Three times a week, I'd drag myself out of bed at 6 a.m., and run in the cold and the dark, three laps, before I went to work. There were several regular characters I saw in the park, who I never actually introduced myself to, because doing that at six in the morning in the dark in a city of several million people would be weird. So we just kind of passed each other regularly, more often if we were running different directions. The lady who faster than me while pushing a jogging stroller with a baby in it. The guy with the two dogs who always dressed like he was going out during a blizzard, only his eyes visible under all his layers. The guy who ran with his arms, hands, and fingers pointed straight down like they were fins (and was also faster than me).

I did my laps, running like a guy who maybe once knew how to run but had sort of forgotten. I also ran like a guy who'd packed on a few extra pounds and watched his cardiovascular fitness fade since high school. I looked like these guys and felt like these guys, my feet thumping the earth where a "real runner" would have glided across it. Up the hill past the condo towers, through the trees between the back entrance to the Botanic Gardens and the marble Parthenon where people got married sometimes, down the hill, around the corner and along 8th Avenue, then up the other side of the park past the condos and the mansion I jokingly called Xanadu after Citizen Kane's estate, across 12th and around the corner to close the loop and start another lap, or, mercifully, if it was the end of my third lap, walk home and shower before heading to work.

I didn't know what I was doing or why I was doing it. I just knew I was doing it.

In studies to see how lab rats' brains react to drugs, researchers have given the rats choices between water, water with sugar, and water laced with a drug like cocaine. They've found that rats, like humans, enjoy drugs—to the point where if they are allowed to self-dose, they up their dosage more and more, and then go through withdrawal when access to the drug-laced water is taken away. For years, the results of these studies were viewed as proving that, like humans, rats were capable of becoming addicted to drugs.

In the early 1980s, however, a researcher named Simon Alexander wondered if maybe the unnatural lab environment housing rats contributed to their drug usage. So he and his colleagues created something they called "Rat Park," which was much larger than a standard rat cage, with brightly colored painted murals, and objects and terrain for the rats to climb and play on. And, perhaps most importantly, the rats were placed in Rat Park in groups of 16 or 20, so they could socialize and interact with other rats.

The rats were given access to drugs, but chose drugs at a much lower rate than their counterparts who lived alone in small, unnatural cages, suggesting that rats who have access to more natural environments, as well as others to socialize with, are less likely to become addicted to drugs.

In her 2011 book *The Lab Rat Chronicles*, Dr. Kelly Lambert writes about Rat Park[3], and another study exploring the effects of nicotine on rats. Rats who had become addicted to nicotine were given a drug that blocked the brain's nicotine receptors. Their brains, unable to receive nicotine, increased production of stress hormones in the amygdala, causing anxiety-like behavior. Lambert writes:

Thus it is likely that the uncomfortable stress response plays a big role in driving the most well-intentioned person trying to kick the cigarette habit toward that pack of cigarettes. ... according to the rats, another effective treatment strategy for addiction is to engage in fulfilling lifestyles (perhaps Human Park?) that decrease the likelihood of consuming drugs in the first place.

The Saturday of my longest training run, I loitered while eating breakfast, procrastinating my 22-mile effort that I just knew was going to take me all day. I drank the last sips of coffee, by that time cold, and when I ran out of excuses, I drove to Denver's Washington Park, where I'd decided to figuratively roll my boulder up the mountain, running laps around the 2.5-mile crushed-rock track for four hours or so. I borrowed my girlfriend's MP3 player to help deal with the boredom. I loaded the MP3 player with some music, mostly Fela Kuti stuff, figuring the rhythms of the long Afrobeat tracks would be approximately the pace of my running/shuffling.

I had, over the course of four months that felt like two years, worked my way up to running 10 miles all at once, then 12 miles, then 15. Finally, a few weeks before the marathon, I'd try 22 miles. I wore a belt with four water bottles on it, stopping a couple times at water fountains on the north and south ends of the park to refill, and begrudgingly lapped the park over and over.

I realized one important thing: Running with music playing in my ears didn't help me. It just made me hate the music. I did not want to ruin Fela Kuti. So I stopped listening to music as I ran.

I also quit running at the 20-mile mark, figuring my body wouldn't know the difference between 20 and 22 miles.

The day of the inaugural Colfax Marathon in 2006, I didn't apply sunscreen to my legs. I didn't think about how they'd be exposed to straight-on sunlight for almost the entire course, which, that first year of the race, went almost completely in an east-to-west straight line along Colfax Avenue, taking two small detours through the Fitzsimmons medical campus in Aurora and through City Park in Denver. I was almost late to the starting line because I neglected to factor in road closures when estimating our drive time. My girlfriend got me as close as she could in her Honda Civic, and I bolted out the passenger door and jogged to the start area, adding another half-mile or so to the longest running day of my life.

A few minutes later, the blob of hundreds of runners started flowing through the start gates, and I shuffled along, trying to keep myself moving slowly.

Years later, I would realize that it was an extremely boring race course, but as it was my first marathon, I was mostly focused on worrying about shin splints or some sort of foot injury that would keep me from finishing the race and rendering moot all those early, cold, dark mornings of hating running around Cheesman Park.

I finished in 4:55:05. I got 40th place out of 48 runners in the Men's 25-to-29-year-old division. I ate an entire pint of Ben & Jerry's Phish Food when I got home.

People run marathons for many reasons: to raise money for charities like the American Cancer Society, to raise awareness for causes, in memory of a loved one who passed away, even to win. The 50 States Marathon Club, created to challenge runners to complete a marathon race in each of the 50 U.S. States has more than 5,000 members who have done so. People want to see if they have what it takes, or run with a friend or family member as a way to share a goal and hopefully a fun memory. To most people, the marathon distance of 26.2 miles seems like a huge number. That's because it is.

I did not, while basking in the glow and endorphins of finishing a marathon, and seeing all that hard work pay off, get hooked on running. I viewed it as a life experience that I had completed, like skydiving, or getting food poisoning, and checked it off my list.

I did buy a new pair of running shoes afterward, doing the thing where you go to a running store and someone watches you run on a treadmill to analyze your gait and fits you with the perfect pair of shoes for your stride. That pair of shoes lasted several years, preserved in a dark corner of my bedroom closet.

I never smoked another cigarette, though.

In March 2010, in a hotel room somewhere in Louisiana, my friend Tony tossed a hardcover book onto my bed as we packed up our stuff to load onto our touring bikes to continue pedaling across the United States. We had left San Diego on February 5 and pedaled an average of 60 miles a day for more than a month. Most people would call it a "bike tour," but it felt like a bit of an endurance event. Tony had a new business back in Chicago and was fairly motivated to finish the trip quickly and get back to work, and I was just along for the ride. We carried all our stuff in trailers attached to our bikes, meaning I had carefully considered the weight of everything in my trailer. So when Tony presented me with a heavy, bulky book, I said, "Whoa, a hardcover?"

It weighed almost a pound and a half. The book was Christopher McDougall's *Born to Run: A Hidden Tribe, Superathletes, and the Greatest Race the World Has Never Seen*.

In the early- to mid-2010s, if you saw someone running barefoot in the park, or while wearing the shoes with separate compartments for each toe, or while wearing minimalist huarache sandals, *Born to Run* was probably responsible. Christopher McDougall would later say in interviews that the point of the book was not that everyone should be running barefoot, but that we should consider our stride and how we impact the ground when we run.

The book was full of interesting ultrarunning characters, one of whom, Micah True, had a simple mantra detailing how one should approach running, in order of priority: Easy, Light, Smooth, Fast.

This was, to me, some revolutionary shit. When our bike trip ended, I got home and ran slowly—ahem, Easy—for an hour straight on a bike path.

I ran a bit, off and on, around Cheesman Park in Denver, but every weekend I could get away, I went rock climbing in the mountains west of Denver, because it felt way more exciting than grinding out laps around the park.

Later that year, I called climber and writer Kelly Cordes to interview him about the idea of being "hardcore." Early on in our phone call, I listed off a few things he had done, big high-altitude mountaineering expeditions in South America and Pakistan, during which he and his partner ran out of food and water and barely survived. I said, "Kelly, that's pretty hardcore, don't you think?"

He humbly replied that no, no, he wasn't that hardcore. But do you know who was? Ultrarunners. In climbing, he said, it's easy to get yourself into a situation where you have no choice but to keep moving—because there's no option to be rescued. If you don't keep moving, you'll die. But an ultramarathon race is different.

"I look at my ultramarathoner friends—OK, so they're running like 100 miles, voluntarily," Kelly said. "So once you start hurting halfway through, and everybody hurts, there's no way anyone feels good for 100 miles—why not just quit? You know, seriously. Why not just call it good at the aid station, sit down, snap your fingers and call for a beer and a bag of chips and say 'I'm done, my legs are tired.' You know, that will to keep going when you have no reason to, that, in a sense, that's actually way hardcore. I think in some ways way more hardcore than situations where you really don't have a choice but to continue."

I met Kelly's friend Craig at a coffee shop in Fort Collins a couple years later. He was the first ultrarunner I ever met in person. He was not a professional runner, or winner of races or anything, just a guy who had run 100 miles all at once.

Over coffee at the Alley Cat, Craig told me that he had chronic pain, thanks to several surgeries, including two spinal fusions, one of which was to repair the first one, which had come apart while he was rock climbing. (The first one was from a surfing accident.) Because of the chronic pain, he was unable to sit in a chair for very long, so as he was studying for CPA exams, he said, he'd get up every couple hours and crank out a half-hour or so on a NordicTrack.

"You mean a NordicTrack, like the old cross-country ski machines that had all those infomercials back in the 90s?"

"Yeah," he said. "They actually do a great job of mimicking running." He eventually wore out lots of the parts, and had to track down replacements.

All the half-hours here and there added up, and on weekends, like most ultrarunners, Craig would make time for a long trail run. But his idea, it seemed, wasn't necessarily total miles of running, but lots of time on your feet.

When Takeru Kobayashi began his career in competitive eating, the world record for hot dogs eaten by one human being in 12 minutes was 25 1/8. That's hot dogs, with buns. When Kobayashi entered the Nathan's Hot Dog Eating Contest in 2001, it had been going for almost 40 years, and was still an eating contest. But Kobayashi, who is 5 feet 8 inches and 130 pounds, viewed competitive eating as a sport. So he trained for it like it was a sport, practicing, experimenting with training methods, tracking what worked and what didn't, and developing new techniques, like ripping the hot dogs and buns in half and soaking the buns in water before shoving them into his mouth.

When he showed up to the contest in 2001, he ate 50 hot dogs in 12 minutes, blowing every contestant out of the water, and setting a new world record—by almost double. What made Kobayashi different? Up until that point, everyone just believed that humans were only capable of eating somewhere around 20 hot dogs in 12 minutes. Kobayashi did not. In a 2014 interview with Stephen Dubner on the *Freakonomics* podcast, Kobayashi said, through translator Maggie James:

"I think the thing about human beings is that they make a limit in their mind of what their potential is. They decide 'I've been told this, or this is what society tells me,' or they've been made to believe something."

Kobayashi's new record was basically the four-minute mile of competitive eating—people thought it was impossible for years, and then someone finally did it, and then more people did it. Kobayashi won six straight Nathan's Hot Dog Eating Contests, until Joey Chestnut won in 2007, eating 67 hot dogs to Kobayashi's 63. From Kobayashi's win in 2001 onward, the lowest winning total has been 44.5—a number thought impossible prior to 2000.[4]

At the finish line of my first marathon in 2006, if someone had offered me $100 to run five more miles, I would have laughed and politely declined before hobbling to my girlfriend's car and going home to sit on the couch and eat an entire pint of Ben & Jerry's. If they offered me $10,000, I would have perked up, but considered it impossible—not humanly impossible, but impossible for me to complete. The race I had just finished, 26.2 miles, was the farthest I had ever run, and as far as I was concerned, was the absolute limit of how far I could ever run. I could not have imagined running five more miles in any situation that didn't involve someone holding a loaded gun to my head.

I had accepted a clearly defined limit of what was possible, and 26.2 miles was it. If someone had run past me at the finish line and told me they were running a 50-mile ultramarathon, I would have, much like the competitors in the 2001 Nathan's Hot Dog Eating Contest watching Takeru Kobayashi, been dumbfounded, without a proper frame of reference to comprehend what I was seeing.

After finishing my first marathon, I took a break from running races for nine years. It seemed to me—and this is not true for everyone—that with marathons and road running, the main storyline was how fast you could get. For whatever reason, the idea of running fast on roads just didn't excite me.

One October Saturday in 2012, I was about 140 feet up a rock climb in southern Utah's red rock desert, standing on a sandstone ledge about the size of the roof of a Toyota Corolla, nursing a ball of mild dread in my gut, ready to turn around and head home even though we hadn't climbed to the top of Castleton Tower like we'd planned. As my partner Chris had climbed above me, a flake of rock had come loose, fell about 40 feet, hit the wall, and broke into chunks above my head. A few of them landed on the pile of rope next to me, cutting it in several places.

We arguably had enough rope left to finish the final 300 feet of the route, but for months already, I had been wondering if I wanted to climb anymore. When I'd started six years ago, I loved it because it scared me, and it helped me learn how to push past fear, I thought. And then, at some point, it became a thing that I was just anxious about, until it was over.

As Chris and I discussed our options, the leader of a pair of young climbers passed us, and then, about 25 feet above, he popped off the wall. Two seconds later, he slammed into the ledge next to us, face-first, which immediately sent him into a seizure.

We, along with other climbers and his partner, spent hours making him comfortable and helping organize a rescue, which ended with him being helicoptered off the saddle below and us walking back to our car in the dark. He ended up fully recovering from the accident, but my passion for climbing didn't. I had watched what could happen when things went wrong, and although I knew accidents like that were rare, I never quite shook it off.

II.

Jayson and I met working in the Applebee's restaurant in Cedar Falls, Iowa, in college, in 1999. We got along immediately because we both liked to tell stories, party, and talk shit to each other. And Jayson had some stories. My significant, even notable, adolescent small-town hell-raising seemed tame in comparison to Jayson's time growing up in Burlington, Iowa, on the Mississippi River. He got in fights, his friends sold drugs and got arrested, they wrecked cars, went to jail. In one of my favorite stories Jayson ever told me, someone's mom hauled off and punched him in the face at a late-night restaurant, because when she insulted his mother, he insulted her back. The police arrived, arrested the woman, and she missed her son's high school graduation ceremony because she was in jail.

We never played pool, or darts, or watched football games on TV. We just sat down and started talking, and other people joined, and the stories just flowed. I'm sure we were way less cool and way more annoying than we thought we were, but at the time, it was the most fun I'd ever had. As we grew out of being idiot partiers into our 20s, we stayed friends, and a darker narrative about Jayson's childhood came to light: a father who abused, then abandoned, the family of six kids; Jayson's dyslexia; bullying at school because of the dyslexia; and generally low expectations for him from every authority figure he met.

He put himself through community college, then college, and then started working political campaigns, where he had a reputation for thinking differently and working his ass off. The thesis of his entire life was dogged persistence: he might not have the exact right tools for the job, but he would get it done, somehow.

I was not surprised when he decided to try ultrarunning.

Our first trail run was just outside of Denver, probably seven or eight miles, up a dirt road that climbed steeply through high-desert grasses and shrubs. Our friend Nick was with us, and all three of us huffed and puffed as the road got steeper, no one wanting to be the one to suggest we walk the rest of the way to the top. If you made it to the top, you'd finished the worst part of the run, and the rest was pretty much flat or downhill, aside from a couple spots where the trail climbed a few dozen feet, so you could hang on for the last six miles or so. Smarter people might have chosen a flatter trail for their first forays into trail running, but we continued to go back to the hilly routes every few weeks, learning that it was more efficient to just walk the steep uphills.

I don't think I was nearly as enamored with it as Jayson was, or at least not as motivated to dive in deep.

Still, when he started talking about entering an ultramarathon, it made sense. It was like going fishing with a friend a few times every summer and then one day, when they come to pick you up, they're towing a boat they just bought behind their car. Of course you're going to get in the car with them.

Jayson's first ultra race, the Bear Chase Race, was in Lakewood, at Bear Creek Lake Park, an oasis of open space sandwiched between a golf course, a four-lane highway, and two freeways. The park is the last bit of flat-ish high desert before the foothills to the Rocky Mountains begin in earnest, with trails winding through prairie grasses and bits of forest. There were three ultramarathon events: A 50K, or 31 miles; a 50-mile race; and a 100K, or 62-mile race. All the races followed a 12.5-mile loop through the park, and runners passed two aid stations on the course as they made their way around to the start/finish area to finish each loop.

It was a 20-minute drive from downtown Denver, and with a loop course, you could stash as much stuff as you thought you needed at the start/finish line, only going 12.5 miles in between changing your socks, or taping blisters, or seeing friends and family. As ultramarathons go, it was very beginner-friendly. That's the case Jayson made when he signed himself up for the 50K race. He had been increasing his longest-distance trail runs for weeks, and he felt good. I was excited for him.

A few weeks before the race, he went into the Denver REI to buy a pair of compression socks, hoping they'd help get him through the longest run he'd ever done. The sales associate in the shoe department who helped him said something like, "You might as well do the 50-mile race," so Jayson went home and changed his registration, nervous but optimistic he could finish four 12.5-mile loops.

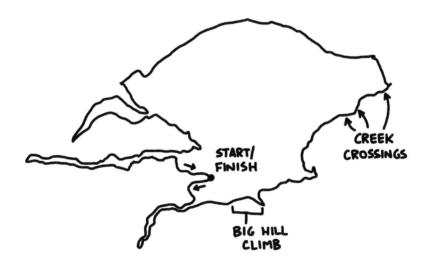

On a Saturday evening with 24 days to go until the Bear Chase Trail Race, my girlfriend Hilary and I met Jayson for deep-dish pizza in Denver's Uptown neighborhood. He had run 27 miles that day, and had earned the calories. I had not run 27 miles that day, but I too believed I deserved that pizza.

While we waited for our food to arrive, Jayson, basking in the runner's high from his marathon-plus trail run earlier in the day, told us how it went: Good at first, but then it got hot. He had stashed some water and food in his car at the trailhead parking lot, and had done several looping routes to run by the car and refill water and food every so often. But on the last loop, he had misjudged, and ran out of water a few miles from the car. He was overheating in full summer Colorado sun and the dry air, and had been moving for hours. He wasn't going to die, but it was not pleasant. He ended up asking some passing hikers if they could spare some water, and they helped him out.

The entire time he told the story, he was half-laughing. It was more ridiculous than serious, like How Did I Get Myself Into This, what an idiot. It sounded … fun?

Fifteen years or so after our first days sitting next to each other on barstools, Jayson was telling me another story, and I was reeled in. I had a creeping feeling that I wanted to be part of the fun. Or "fun," as it were.

The next morning, after some coffee, I decided to run 10 miles around our neighborhood, just to see how it felt. Had I run nine miles, or even seven miles, recently? No I had not. I just figured if my legs held together and nothing broke in 10 miles, maybe I'd think about signing up for the Bear Chase Race 50K.

I mean, it was only 4.8 miles longer than a marathon. And I'd run a marathon before. Nine years ago. When I was much younger. And after lots of training. And I'd also hated the actual running of the marathon.

I ran loops on the sidewalks around Capitol Hill, and I felt mostly OK, besides being tired. I waited 24 hours, then signed up for the Bear Chase Trail Race 50K.

I bought an ultrarunning vest, basically a very lightweight, minimal backpack that had enough room for two water bottles on the chest and some snacks, plus maybe a jacket in the back pocket. I mapped out a 7.5-mile loop on the trails around Green Mountain, the closest place to my house with singletrack trails and a little elevation gain. I put some extra food and water in the car, closed the hatch, and took off at a conservative jogging pace, promising myself I'd hike all of the uphill parts. Forty feet from the car, the trail started to climb up to a freeway overpass, and I went ahead and jogged it instead of walking. I was already breathing hard a couple hundred strides later, but kept running across the overpass until I hit singletrack. And then I started walking the uphill parts.

I did one loop, walking the uphills and jogging everything else, then stopped back at the car and refilled my water bottles. I did another loop, same thing, and didn't feel too bad, considering it was basically a half-marathon plus two miles. I stopped back at the car again, filled up one water bottle, and hiked and ran two more miles in one direction, then turned around and headed back to the car. I had been moving for a little over four hours—definitely not speedy, but I had kept hiking and running almost the entire time, minus refilling water bottles and a couple bathroom stops. And as far as I could tell, I wasn't injured. Could I do 12 more miles in a couple weeks? I was not confident.

The next week, I went back to Green Mountain with a plan: Same loop, three times, no walking, which would be 22.5 miles. By the time I started my third lap, it was 80 degrees, and there was no shade. My legs hurt, the muscles holding that I've-been-standing-all-day fatigue. And then, random weird pains: First my right shin hurt for a mile, then my left arch. Then my right Achilles tendon hurt for a couple miles, then it went away. I assumed this is how it went with these types of things, and that I would know when something hurt enough to be serious. I kept up a 13-minute-per-mile pace, running all the hills this time.

I finished 22.5 miles without walking. I didn't break anything. I had some chafing, and my legs felt the same ache they'd felt back when I was a bartender and I worked a double shift, standing on my feet pouring drinks and delivering food for nine to 12 hours. I was probably extremely dehydrated, since I hadn't peed since sometime during my first lap. But I could still walk.

I have a recurring dream every few months or so, in which I am walking around a college campus, and I realize that I registered for a class at the beginning of the semester, but I have somehow forgotten to attend a single class session. In the dream, it's late in the semester, and final exams are approaching, and I somehow still have some hope that I can catch up on the course material and do OK on the final exam for the class I have never attended.

A quick Google search for the words "training plan for 50K ultra" would have pulled up several free training schedules from professional running coaches. The problem with those training plans is that they all start around 24 to 26 weeks before race day.

If I had done this Google search the day I signed up for the Bear Chase Trail Race 50K, and then synced my calendar with a 24-week training plan, I would have been in the middle of Week 21.

I'm sure if I had asked a running coach for their opinion, they would have advised me to sign up for a different race later in the year, so I could give myself the time to train and be ready for it and perform better in said race. Which certainly would have been smart advice.

Hilary and I were about five minutes into watching *Atomic Blonde* when she said "I can't do this," which was her way of saying "we can watch a different movie together, or you can watch the rest of this movie by yourself."

She was not being unreasonable. In the opening five minutes, a man is brutally killed, first after being hit by a car and then shot, in a very realistic-looking (and sounding) scene.

I started thinking about how I was so much more used to violence in movies than she was. I have watched probably 300 or so action movies in my life, in which thousands of people had been beaten, stabbed, shot, and killed. If we were to interpret the action movie star as a model for a modern-day hero, usually the most heroic thing someone could do is kill someone else who is trying to harm the hero, and/or the hero's family, and/or innocent people.

When I sit down and try to find a movie to watch, I usually feel like I am deciding between two types of movies:

GOOD VS. EVIL	OTHER
• FROM EARLY ON, YOU KNOW WHO THE "GOOD GUYS" ARE • YOU FIND YOURSELF "ROOTING" FOR ONE "SIDE" • ONE SIDE "WINS" IN THE END	• CHARACTERS MAY NOT BE EASILY CLASSIFIED AS "GOOD" OR "EVIL" • STORY IS USUALLY MORE NUANCED/LESS STRAIGHTFORWARD • THERE MAY BE MORE THAN TWO "SIDES," AND YOU MAY NOT BE "ROOTING" FOR ANYONE • NO CLEAR "WINNER" OR "LOSER" AT END

Of course there are more than two types of movies, but for the most part, I'm trying to decide what I want to do with my brain and emotions: Good vs. Evil movies are easy, and Other movies are hard. I either get to shut my brain off (Good vs. Evil) or I watch a movie (Other) that forces me to think during and afterward (sometimes for days or weeks): Was the narrator reliable? Why did Character X do that? Why did the filmmakers include the second-to-last scene? Which character do I identify with? What did the ending mean (to me)?

Good vs. Evil is a compelling storyline, and is a very direct way to stir up emotion, and even motivation. When I was in junior high watching my heroes on our town's high school basketball team playing in a packed gym, I found players on the other team to detest. The more points they scored, the more I hated them. I hated the way they released a jump shot, or used their elbows, or their haircut, or their shoes, or their acne. Not only were they unlikable for coming to our town and having the gall to score points against our team, they were also probably horrible, evil people in their non-basketball lives.

Later in life, I picked politicians to side with, and despised politicians I saw as being on "the other side." Lots of people do this. It's easier to see the world in black and white, with no nuance. You're either with us or you're against us. Sometimes there are no real enemies, and we just make them up.

Author Nir Eyal has written about how people, most notably, mega-successful musician DJ Khaled, will go so far as to create imaginary enemies to motivate themselves:[5]

DJ Khaled, the one-man internet meme, is known for warning his tens of millions of social media followers about a group of villains he calls "they."

"They don't want you motivated. They don't want you inspired," he blares on camera. "They don't want you to win," he warns. On Ellen DeGeneres's talk show, Khaled urged the host, "Please, Ellen, stay away from them!"

The "they" Khaled invokes are clearly a sinister force. But who are they? Khaled offered clues when he told DeGeneres, "They are the people who don't believe in you....They is the person that told you you would never have an Ellen show."

Although Khaled's claims may seem outlandish, he is in fact leveraging a powerful psychological hack: scapegoating. The practice of imagining a villain that's conspiring against us, scapegoating can be an effective way to motivate ourselves and change our behaviors.

When we hear the word "race" in regards to running, we of course think of an event in which everyone is trying to run faster than the other entrants. That's because this is literally the definition of the word "race":

race

noun (2)

1a: a competition between people, animals, vehicles, etc., to determine which one is the fastest : a contest of speed

I couldn't put my finger on why I wanted to try ultramarathons, but I definitely wasn't getting my hopes up to be anywhere near the fastest person out there. I was just curious if I could cover 31 miles in one day, and see what it was like, how it felt, and who these other people were who did this sort of thing for fun. I didn't care if I got dead last. The only thing I was worried about was finishing before the 10½-hour cutoff. I had run 22.5 miles in about five hours, so if I could get anywhere near that on the race day, barring a major injury, I would have about five more hours to cover the final 8.5 miles.

I was pretty sure I was not a real runner, or even a real trail runner. But my rationale was: I had spent some long days on my feet in the mountains while doing other things, like backpacking and rock climbing, both requiring hours of hiking while wearing a backpack weighing anywhere from 15 to 40 pounds. I definitely hadn't covered 31 miles on my feet in one day before, but I'd been on my feet for 12 to 14 hours. I'd had days of waiting tables longer than 10½ hours. Was it dumb to think of all this as preparation? Maybe. Was I being that guy at the office who lacks experience and knowledge and gets by on sheer fake-it-till-you-make-it bullshit that he tells himself and everyone else? I mean, I would not say I was sleeping well the week before the race. So I wasn't even successful at bullshitting myself.

I was just going to try it, and see. The worst thing that could happen was failure—being unable to finish, or missing the cutoff.

Actually, failure plus an injury was probably the worst thing that could happen. And I guess there's always the possibility of having gastrointestinal problems. So failure, plus injury, plus pooping my pants in front of a bunch of strangers.

A few nights before I would run the Bear Chase Trail Race in Colorado, a comedian named Matt Little was 1,600 miles away, headed home from his job at the Upright Citizens Brigade Theater on Manhattan's Lower East Side, dead tired. As he walked down the stairs to the 1st Avenue L subway stop, he saw a rat carrying a full-size slice of pizza down the stairs. He pulled his phone out of his pocket and recorded a 15-second video of the rat, dragging a slice almost three times the size of its body, scurrying down the concrete steps.

Little thought nothing of it, until the next morning, when he was scrolling through his phone looking for another video, and watched it again. He uploaded it to Instagram and YouTube, and it went viral. By evening, the "Pizza Rat" clip was being shown on national late-night shows. In 24 hours, the video had more than 2 million views on YouTube and Instagram[6]. The video inspired dozens of jokes, fictional stories about the rat, and theories about why people loved it so much.

"It's all a metaphor for living in New York," Little told BuzzFeed News[7]. "You have too far to go and too much carry. But life gives you as much as you can handle."

A CNN.com article[8] paraphrased the phenomenon with a succinct sub-headline: "We are all Pizza Rat, social media proclaims."

The day of the race, the weather forecast called for sunny skies and 85-degree high temperatures. Shade on the race course was not plentiful—maybe 30 percent of the route, total—so it would be a hot day for seven to 10.5 hours of cardio.

At the start line, 120 runners milled about, dressed in brightly colored shorts, T-shirts, singlets, and running vests, exhibiting various proportions of nervous-to-excited, trying to stretch, cram food in their vest and shorts pockets, and perhaps summon a last-minute bowel movement.

A handful of people looked like they might be there to win, with the physique of what you might call a "real runner": lean, sinewy, everything dialed, carrying almost nothing with them—maybe a water bottle at most. They knew what they were doing, while those of us with full-on running vests might be packing our anxieties in our various pockets—certain foods we knew wouldn't give us digestion trouble, Body Glide, some tape, Band-Aids, Imodium, ibuprofen, smartphones. Most of us just looked like the people you see jogging around the park on a weekend morning or weekday afternoon—hobbyists with more than 10 percent body fat, maybe a little overdressed in one way or another, maybe nervously talking and joking with anyone who would listen, maybe not 100 percent sure of what kind of shoes to wear for a race like this, maybe doing this distance for the first time ever. Like me.

I had told myself to just walk the first two minutes of the race, instead of wasting energy trying to keep up with a whole pack of excited runners. There was no reason to go fast at the beginning—I was going to be out here for six hours at the absolute minimum, so shaving off a few seconds by running fast at the beginning would not only be a waste of energy, it would also be dumb.

But then everyone started jogging through the starting arch so I started jogging too, and by the half-mile mark, I found myself passing people on a slight uphill, literally doing the exact opposite of my conservative plan. By the time we started Mile 4, everyone had started to spread out a bit and I could settle in to my own pace.

Well, everybody does something, usually anyway. So we thought we would do this and it would be fun.

Professional athletes do not usually eat during games. If you can find a video of an NBA or NFL player actually consuming food on the sidelines, they are actively trying to hide it from cameras—like New York Jets quarterback Mark Sanchez sitting down on the bench behind a line of players to eat a hot dog during a 2012 game against the Oakland Raiders, or Steph Curry during a Golden State Warriors game, hiding a banana behind a towel between hasty bites. LeBron James was not shy about snacking on Red Vines on the bench after scoring 40 points against the New Orleans Pelicans in 2020, and it was news: Business Insider and USA Today wrote about it, and clips of it made their way around Twitter.

Basketball games, football games, and baseball games take two to three hours. NBA players burn between 600 and 1,000 calories during a game, depending on playing time. Professional soccer players in a 90-minute game burn between 1,500 and 2,000 calories. Marathon runners can burn anywhere from 1,500 to 2,500 calories during a race, depending on their weight and how fast they finish—elite marathoners usually finish in just over two hours, and the average finish time for NYC Marathon finishers in 2019 was 4:39:02. Ultramarathons can last anywhere from three hours to several days. Most races between 50K and 100 miles, however, have cutoff times between 10 and 36 hours.

Dean Karnazes' bestselling book *Ultramarathon Man* begins not during one of his many ultramarathon races around the world, but as he's making a phone call while running alone at night near Petaluma, California, partway through a 199-mile run from Calistoga, California, to Santa Cruz. As he's trotting along, he's on the phone with the manager of Family Table, ordering a pizza. And a cherry cheesecake. Which he wants delivered while he's on the move, so he doesn't have to stop. The delivery driver meets him at a dark highway intersection and takes off, leaving him jogging with an armful of food[9]:

With the cheesecake stacked on top of the pizza, I started running again, eating as I went. Over the years I'd perfected the craft of eating on the fly. I balanced the box of pizza and cheesecake in one hand and ate with the other. It was a good upper-body workout. Fortunately, my forearms were well developed and had no problem supporting the added weight. For efficiency, I rolled four pieces of pizza into one big log like a huge Italian burrito. Easier to fit in my mouth that way.

The first aid station of my first ultramarathon was a revelation. The 50K (31 miles) route of trails was punctuated with seven aid stations, or one every four and a half miles. Every time I passed one, if I needed to stop, volunteers greeted me, asking "What can we get you?" and "How are you doing?" They held out their hands to grab my water bottles to refill them with water or electrolyte drinks. There were tables laid out with peanut butter and jelly sandwiches, bean burritos, pickles, pretzels, M&M's, Peanut M&M's, Skittles, Chips Ahoy!, Oreos, vanilla wafers, electrolyte drinks. Nice people stood by, ready to hand me all of these things. And every aid station on the course was like this—a small buffet of junk food along a trail, with friendly volunteers to help you and subtly nudge you to keep going.

MARATHON AID STATION	ULTRAMARATHON AID STATION
WATER	WATER
ELECTROLYTE DRINK	ELECTROLYTE DRINK
MAYBE BANANAS	OREOS
	POTATO CHIPS
	M&M's
	SKITTLES
	PRETZELS
	PICKLES
	PB+Js CUT IN ¼s
	COCA-COLA
	SOMETIMES: PANCAKES, QUESADILLAS, BACON, COFFEE, WHISKEY, PIZZA

I ran the first lap a little fast, then finished the second lap feeling pretty good. I passed a few people here and there, but I had no idea where I was in relation to other 120 people in the 50K, because we shared the course with the 50-mile runners and the 100K runners. I tried to run all the parts of the trail that weren't significantly uphill. I reminded myself to eat 100 calories or so every half-hour, pulling gels and CLIF BLOKS from my vest, and supplementing with cookies from the aid stations. It was hot in the sun, and I was sweating a lot. I tried to keep myself to an "all-day" pace, pumping the brakes early on when I wanted to run fast—but after about the halfway point, the fatigue in my under-trained legs started pumping the brakes for me.

I began the second lap, jogging Mile 18.5, feeling tired, but optimistic. My legs ached, I had sweated out a lot of fluids but had drunk enough water to keep from getting a headache, and I had hours until the final cutoff.

At about Mile 26, I coasted downhill into the aid station, congratulating myself that this was my last visit here. In five more miles, I'd be done. I grabbed a couple cookies and decided to let myself walk while I munched on them. As soon as I finished, I took the first steps into my shuffle-run to finish the race.

A sharp pain shot into the side of my right knee. I shifted my weight to my left leg, then tried to run another step with my right leg. Same pain. Big pain. I tried to keep moving, wincing a little bit with each right-leg step. It hurt to jog. Wow, it hurt to walk. I tried a slow lunge forward, then tried pulling my foot up behind my hamstring to stretch it out. No relief. I limped forward, still trying to take steps, hobbling away from the aid station. This was not one of those little aches and pains; this was an injury, wasn't it?

I was about two hundred feet from the aid station. I halfway turned on the trail. Maybe I should go back. Call it a day. It was real pain. I should not have been surprised. This is what happens when you do something dumb, like trying to run an ultramarathon more or less off the couch.

What happens if I quit here? Do they send someone to pick me up? Do they call my girlfriend to come and get me? I couldn't even remember her phone number. The logistics seemed too complicated. I didn't want to be a burden to people.

I turned back on the trail and kept walking forward. I could walk just fine. I'll just walk the last five miles. Worst case, that would take an hour and a half or two hours. As long as the pain didn't get any worse.

After a hundred steps or so, the trail started a small climb. I jogged a few steps. Hm. Was it my IT band? Not that I knew what that is, but people—runners—talked about them. I stopped and dug my fingers into the side of my thigh, pushing hard and rubbing up and down. Then the heel of my hand. I took a step. That felt a little better, didn't it? I walked, then started jogging again. The trail turned downhill. I jogged, sharp pain, stopped, walked. OK, no running on the downhills, then.

I walked the flats and uphills most of the next mile and a half, then jogged the last half mile to the final aid station, 3.2 miles from the finish. I massaged my IT band, or where I thought it was, as hard as I could, then started running the last section. I felt OK. I shuffle-ran the last three miles through the forest, figuring I'd kick it in and try to actually look like I was running for the last 500 feet or so to the finish line. It was OK. My knee was going to make it. No telling what would happen when I sat down for a few minutes after the race, but for now, it seemed like it wasn't serious.

Hilary jumped up from her seat about 400 feet from the finish and jogged in next to the trail as I picked up the pace a little bit—no sense sprinting, I figured. Plus I wasn't too confident that I wouldn't come apart like Herbie the Love Bug if I pushed too hard.

I had severely underprepared for my first ultra race, and survived, with hopefully no permanent or semi-permanent injuries. Jayson was still out on the race course, metaphorically having jumped into the deep end of the pool, albeit with a lot more training miles on his legs. Our friend Nick had shown up be his official pacer for his last 12.5-mile lap of the course, pinning a bib on his shirt and slowly hiking with Jayson out of the start/finish area.

Nick might have thought he was coming along to glance down at his watch every few seconds and make sure Jayson kept to a certain pace—say 10-minute miles, or 11-minute miles. But as it turned out, his job was closer to that of the friend who was put in charge of making sure Jayson got home from the bar OK on his 21st birthday. A babysitter, for a fully-grown adult who was otherwise capable of taking care of their own normal life functions, except for right now.

76

During Jayson and Nick's final lap, which took more than three hours, Jayson's digestive system was in full revolt, and several areas in his legs were also not happy that he'd forced them to try to ambulate for 50 miles in one day. The sun went down, and we sat in camp chairs and waited, until finally, just after the 13-hour mark, Nick and a shirtless Jayson came through the finish arch, running, not fast, but running—and smiling.

My knee pain turned out to not be a significant injury. It was coming from my iliotibial band, the mystical "IT band" I'd heard rumors of. Lots of runners develop something called iliotibial band syndrome, which essentially happens when the IT band, a ligament running from your pelvis to your shinbone, rubs against your thigh bone:

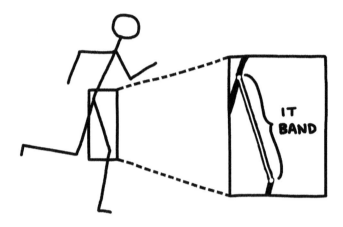

If it becomes chronic, runners will often be able to run a mile or two and feel just fine, and then start feeling pain in the side of the knee or thigh.

I self-diagnosed my knee pain, already knowing that I had done something pretty dumb by trying to run 31 miles with almost zero training. An internet search led me to WebMD, which informed me of some things that typically cause IT band syndrome:

- Not doing enough to stretch, warm up, and cool down

- Pushing too hard—you go too far or for too long

- Not resting long enough between workouts

- Running downhill

If stoking IT band syndrome was a job, I was definitely qualified. Treating and preventing it, however, can be less than straightforward. Some people have luck with stretching, switching to different shoes, ultrasound, massage, ice, working on their running form, and in extremely rare cases, IT band "release" surgery, in which a small piece of the IT band is cut from the ligament where it rubs on the bone.

Or you can quit running, because running is the thing causing it.

A few years before, I had been climbing a mountain in Colorado with my friend Lee in the winter, which is not a good time to be climbing a mountain in Colorado because the weather is generally against you. Most people ski in the winter, at resorts, where ski runs have been cut through huge stands of trees, which mostly shield you from wind. And if you get cold, you can pop into a lodge somewhere and get a hot chocolate. If you're skiing and the weather sucks, most people generally go home, because skiing is supposed to be fun. Mountaineering is not something that's sold to anyone as a "fun" activity. Meaningful, yes, but fun, not so much.

I followed Lee up a ridge on the side of a mountain, and there was no place to hide from the wind, which was blowing snow into our faces. We slogged uphill in heavy boots, trying to breathe in the thinner air at 11,000 feet or so, noses dripping. We were finding lots of meaning in our weekend hobby. Lee said, as he had several times before, "You know what I like about mountaineering? It feels so good when you stop."

This of course is a version of an old joke, in which a man sees another man hitting his thumb repeatedly with a hammer* and asks, "Why are you doing that?" The man with the hammer says, "It feels so good when I stop."

*in another version of the joke, the man does not have a hammer, but is banging his head on the wall

I took a week off of running after the Bear Chase 50K. I did some hiking, and everything felt pretty OK, including my IT band. I ate more than usual the day after the race, my body sending signals that I had burned several thousand calories more than usual and needed to replace them. A few days after the race, I met Jayson for coffee, and he was in much rougher shape, with inflammation in different spots throughout his legs from the shock of covering 50 miles in a day.

After my first marathon, I was satisfied that I had checked something off my life list, and was ready to move on to something else. Now, I had checked an ultramarathon off my list, and strangely, I found myself even more curious. If I handled 31 miles OK, what would 50 miles feel like? It helped that Jayson had done it and survived mostly unscathed.

A few weeks later, we met up for a trail run, and somewhere in the conversation, we started circling each other, talking like two kids standing next to the high dive at the pool, both trying to convince the other one to go first, because they both kind of want to try it, but also they both kind of don't want to try it.

At noon on December 18, Jayson and I opened our laptops and hurriedly signed up for the Ice Age Trail 50-mile race in Wisconsin before all of the 300 spots were filled. The race is one of the oldest continuously-running ultramarathons in the U.S., created in 1981 as the first ultramarathon in the Midwest, and every year, it sold out minutes after online registration opened.

The race was on May 14th, giving me much more time to train this time.

Ideally, in preparing to run a 50-mile race on singletrack trails with lots of ups and downs, I'd like to do a lot of training runs on singletrack trails with lots of ups and downs.

In Colorado's Front Range from December through April, almost all the single-track trails with any elevation gain are covered in snow and ice, and if they're not covered in snow and ice, they're in some stage of melting, meaning they're muddy, and running on those trails can trash them.

We had one dirt road we could run, to the top of Green Mountain, which rises about 850 feet in two miles. Since they regularly drive trucks up the road to service communications equipment at the top, we weren't as worried about ruining it by running on it when it was wet. And we could run on the asphalt road up and over Dinosaur Ridge, essentially across the street from Green Mountain, and then, if it wasn't busy, on some of the narrow paved roads leading up to Red Rocks Amphitheater. None of these would really replicate a singletrack trail with rocks and roots, but I figured all the folks who had entered the race and lived in the Midwest were probably dealing with similar snowy conditions.

Jayson and I would run on our own during the week, then meet up on Saturday or Sunday to do increasingly longer runs on the hills of Green Mountain, Dinosaur Ridge, and Red Rocks. Occasionally we'd get lucky and things were dry, but we often spent our training hours slogging through snow, or running on the shoulders of roads as cars sped by. None of it would have made very good video footage for a running-shoe commercial, but we managed to get in the miles, for the most part, steadily doing 20 miles, 18 miles, 23 miles, 24 miles, 26 miles, and then a 31-mile run four weeks before the race.

Early in the evening before the Ice Age Trail 50, we checked into a hotel in Elkhorn, Wisconsin, and tried to get some sleep before the 6 a.m. start. I had one goal: finish before the 12-hour cutoff. I also had: anxiety. My brain was primed for rumination and cyclical thinking about Everything That Could Go Wrong. A short list of questions I had for the universe:

- What if I don't sleep at all the night before the race?

- What if I oversleep and miss the start of the race?

- What if we can't find a parking spot at the starting line?

- What if I can't execute a successful bowel movement before the start of the race?

- What if I have gastrointestinal distress and can't keep anything down during the race?

- What if I have gastrointestinal distress and everything comes out the other end during the race?

- What if my water bottles start leaking, or my vest breaks, or starts chafing, or my shoes somehow blow out?

- What if I develop blisters?

- What if I didn't bring enough food?

- What if I didn't train enough?

- What if any body part starts hurting so much that I can't continue?

- What if it rains?

- What if it snows?

- What if I can't handle the pain?

- What happens after 31 miles?

You could look around the starting line of an ultramarathon and attempt to generalize about who ultrarunners are, but I think it might be tough to nail down. There are elite athletes and grandparents, people who have run dozens of ultramarathons and people trying it for their first time, people who have found ultrarunning after years of road marathons and people like me, who maybe weren't even runners but just thought it would be interesting. Or "fun."

The average age usually skews a bit older than you might think: The biggest age group in the 2016 Ice Age Trail 50 was age 40-49, with 107 runners. More than two-thirds of the runners were between the ages of 30 and 49. There were twice as many runners in their 50s (51 total) than in their 20s (24). And 16 people in their 60s ran 50 miles that day.

At age 37, I was contributing to the social security benefits being collected by five other people running in the Ice Age Trail 50 with me. Three of them finished ahead of me.

There's a diversity of body shapes, ages, and backgrounds, but most races draw people who are near the middle of their lives. I don't know what that means, but I think if I were to generalize, I'd say lots of ultrarunners are people who got to a certain point in life, wondered what else was out there for them, heard about the idea of running more than 26.2 miles, and thought, "Maybe I could do that too."

I slept some, maybe five or six hours total. ✓

We woke up on time. ✓

I had a timely bowel movement. ✓

We found a parking spot without any problem. ✓

During Mile 2, the outside of my left foot started hurting, in a very new-to-me place. The pain was not catastrophic, just nagging, and I figured it would go away if I just kept going. It did. ✓

It snowed lightly for a few minutes early in the race. ✓

I did not train enough.

My water bottles were fine, my vest held up, I had no abnormal chafing, and my shoes held together just fine. ✓

I had no major gastrointestinal issues, but nearly had an emergency around Mile 43, and made it to a pit toilet in time. In one of the most disgusting things that's ever happened to me in a restroom, the pit toilet splashed me from below—probably due to some water leaking into the reservoir beneath the toilet. At that point in the race, I was so miserable, I just shrugged and cleaned myself up the best as I could and then headed back out.

The race route winds through the forest, making a 10-mile loop near the start/finish area before heading out on a long leg of the Ice Age National Scenic Trail, a 1,200-mile trail snaking across Wisconsin, following the terminal moraine from the last Ice Age. Runners head southwest for about 10 miles, then turn back the way they came to retrace their steps, then keep heading northeast for about 8 miles to a turnaround where they retrace their steps again until about Mile 47, when they finally turn off and finish the final mellow three miles to the finish. The race map looked like this:

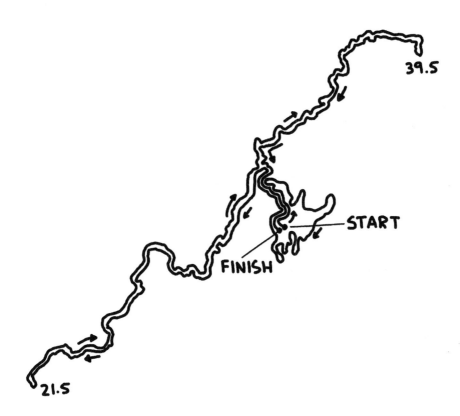

A simplified version of the race map might look like this:

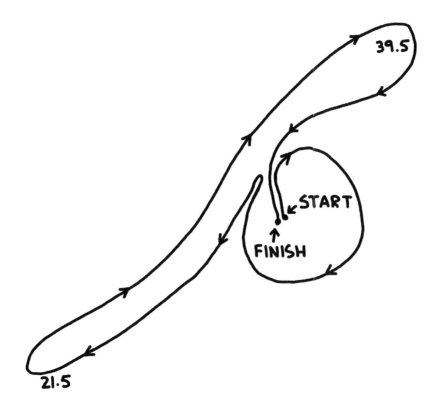

We fell into a pace, and plugged away, walking the uphills, running everything else. But I began to notice a pattern: We would catch up to a runner or group of runners who were walking a section, and wanting to go a little faster, we'd pick up our running speed to pass them, sometimes while going uphill, which seems like a big waste of energy, especially when you're passing three or four people at a time.

There are 10 aid stations along the Ice Age Trail 50 course, and because the course bends back on itself so many times, there are actually 16 opportunities to stop at aid stations, almost one every three miles. We didn't stop at all of them, but every time we did, even if it was just to grab a cookie and keep moving, I swear all the groups of people we had passed earlier somehow ended up in front of us. And we'd pass them again. I couldn't help thinking they were going about the whole thing in a smarter way than we were.

Finally, maybe for the first time in our friendship, I ran out of energy to make conversation with Jayson about 80 percent of the way through the race. The weather had been blissfully cloudy, cool, and gray the entire day, 40 degrees at the starting line. Heatstroke was not an issue, and staying hydrated was much less challenging, since we weren't sweating much.

You might say that the Midwest, compared to Colorado, could be called "flat." It's true that there are no 14,000-foot peaks in the Midwest, and the high point of Wisconsin is not quite 2,000 feet in elevation.

We were coming from Colorado, which you might think would give us an advantage, because we lived and trained in thinner air at a higher elevation. We had done a decent job of training, not doing 100 percent of the miles on a typical schedule, but definitely getting most of the long runs in. And we could, theoretically, train in the mountains.

Colorado and Iowa each have weeklong bicycle tour events, each covering about 500 miles over seven days. In 2011, the website bikingbis.com compared the elevation profile of the two rides. The total elevation gain on Ride the Rockies that year was 21,604 feet. RAGBRAI's total elevation gain that year was 21,206 feet[10]. The routes for each ride change every year—and it was a particularly hilly year for RAGBRAI and a flatter year for Ride the Rockies. But the data showed the Midwest terrain's capacity to deliver the colloquial "death by a thousand papercuts."

I was not surprised to be getting my ass kicked by the Ice Age Trail 50, especially by Mile 40. The last 10 miles started to feel like they were going to break me. My legs hummed with electrical currents of ache, and bringing my knee and foot up to jog a step forward felt like twice the effort it took during any of my training runs. I could not get motivated to run, and would only reluctantly start jogging if I saw Jayson begin running on the trail in front of me. He was not experiencing the 50-mile distance for the first time, and maybe that helped. Also, maybe he's just way tougher than me. It didn't matter. I was just happy he was there.

The hills were not big, but all those 80-foot and 100-foot climbs and descents add up, physically and mentally. Thru-hikers on the Appalachian trail long ago coined the term "PUDs," for "pointless ups and downs." Why does the trail go over this hill? Why does the race course go this way? Why did I sign up for this race? Why did I think any of this was a good idea? Why don't I have a fun hobby that hurts less, like golf? My legs had a constant buzz of aching pain from my hips on down.

Around Mile 47, someone was handing out cake and beer, because it was the 35th anniversary of the race. I took some cake, and it totally changed my outlook, for about 90 seconds.

"I'm done," I told Jayson. "I'm walking in from here." I looked at my watch, and if I walked at a decent clip, I'd finish in just under 12 hours. I wanted to be an ultrarunner, but I was not too proud to walk across the finish line.

With a half-mile to go, we heard cheers from the start/finish area, somewhere through the trees, and we started running. As we rounded the corner and could see a few dozen people at the finish line, Jayson started clapping and cheering and pumping his fists next to me. I managed a weak smile. We crossed the finish line in 11 hours, 26 minutes, and 50 seconds—33 minutes to spare.

Almost all of the most popular sports in the United States—basketball, football, baseball, hockey—have a clearly defined winning team and a losing team at the end of each game. We celebrate winning, and winners, and we align ourselves with them. In a 1976 study[11], psychologist Robert Cialdini found that when our favorite sports team wins, we refer to the team as "we," but when our favorite team loses, we refer to the team as "they." There isn't much room for nuance—one team scored more points than the other team, or they didn't. At the end of the season, there is one champion, and a whole bunch of non-champions.

In the mid-2010s, giving kids participation trophies became controversial. Detractors said they were making kids soft, teaching them to accept mediocrity and to not try hard. Supporters said they taught kids that trying their best, not winning, was what really mattered. Some called Millennials "the participation trophy generation," calling them "entitled" and "lazy." Others said that an award for showing up for practice and games was a good thing, given all the things the kids could be doing otherwise—and that kids were smart enough to know the difference between a first-place trophy and a participation trophy.

Pittsburgh Steelers linebacker James Harrison made his 8-year-old and 6-year-old sons give back the trophies they received for going to a camp, and wrote in an Instagram post in 2015:

"I came home to find out that my boys received two trophies for nothing, participation trophies! While I am very proud of my boys for everything they do and will encourage them till the day I die, these trophies will be given back until they EARN a real trophy. I'm sorry I'm not sorry for believing that everything in life should be earned and I'm not about to raise two boys to be men by making them believe that they are entitled to something just because they tried their best...cause sometimes your best is not enough, and that should drive you to want to do better...not cry and whine until somebody gives you something to shut u up and keep you happy."[12]

After a 2016 loss, Louisville women's basketball head coach Jeff Walz said in a post-game interview:

"Right now, the generation of kids that are coming through, everybody gets a damn trophy, okay? You finish last, you come home with a trophy. You kidding me? What's that teaching kids? It's okay to lose! And unfortunately, it's our society. It's what we're building for.

"And it's not just in basketball, it's in life. Everybody thinks they should get a job. Everybody thinks they should get a good job. No, that's not the way it works. But unfortunately, that's what we are preparing for. Because you finish fifth, you walk home with this nice trophy, parents are all excited? No.

"I mean, not to be too blunt, but you're a loser. Like, we're losers, we got beat. So you lost. There is no trophy for us."[13]

In August 1955, Wendell Robie organized a 100-mile horse ride on trails from Tahoe City, California, over the Sierra Nevada to Auburn, California, where Robie lived. Robie thought it might be possible for a horseback rider to travel 100 miles in 24 hours, and he wanted to try it. Five riders showed up at the starting line, and followed an old mining trail Robie named the "Western States Trail." Four riders finished, with Robie and another rider, Nick Wendell, finishing first in 22 hours and 45 minutes.

The ride, originally named "100 Miles One Day Western States Pony Express Ride," continued on, and in 1959 a trophy called The Tevis Cup was given to the winner. Any rider who finished the route in under 24 hours with a healthy horse was given a sterling silver belt buckle commemorating their finish.

Gordy Ainsleigh started competing in the ride in 1971, often running alongside his horse. In 1972, a group of soldiers from Fort Riley, Kansas, were allowed to enter the race on foot, to see if they could march the 100 miles in 48 hours. Seven of them finished. Ainsleigh rode again in 1972 and finished, and again in 1973, but dropped out after 30 miles when his horse couldn't continue. When the 1974 ride came around, he still hadn't found another horse, and decided to try to run the race. In 107-degree heat, running through the night, and almost quitting at one point, he finished in 23:42, becoming the first person to cover the Western States course on foot in under 24 hours.[14]

In 1977, Robie added a 100-mile run to the event, and a new record was set. In 1978, the run was held separately from the horse ride, and it quickly became the most famous 100-mile trail ultramarathon in the United States, drawing 63 starters in 1978, and 143 starters in 1979.

The Western States 100-Mile Endurance Run continues to be one of the most coveted and most watched races in ultrarunning, with thousands of people entering the lottery for 369 race spots. Runners who finish in under 24 hours are awarded a handmade silver Western States 100 belt buckle. Runners who finish in under 30 hours are awarded a handmade bronze Western States 100 belt buckle.

Western States was the first 100-mile trail race in the world, and in the years that followed, ultrarunning grew. Hundreds of other races, following the lead of Western States, now award belt buckles to runners who finish their races.

Jayson and I plopped down in a couple camp chairs just past the finish line and put on some warmer layers. Sitting down was nearly orgasmic. It quite literally felt so good when I stopped. The ache throughout my legs and feet dissipated over the few seconds following my butt hitting the chair, as if someone was controlling the pain with a dimmer switch. We regrouped for a few minutes, chatting with Hilary and Jayson's brother Jaymes and my parents, taking some time to punctuate our finish, and then got up to get out of the chilly air and head to a restaurant for a post-race meal.

As we hobbled toward our cars in the parking lot, a huge roar of cheers erupted from the start/finish area. I looked back to see what it was about, but we were too far around the corner. The cheering kept on, for 30 seconds, maybe a minute? What was that?

I glanced down at my watch to see it was almost 6:00 p.m. The cheers were for the last runners coming in before the cutoff—one person finished in 11:58:54, and another crossed the line at 11:59:13. If you had just shown up without any idea of what was going on and heard the crowd, you might have thought those two people had won the race.

The next morning, I woke up in the Hampton Inn and as soon as I stood up to walk to the bathroom, that pain in my left foot from Mile 2 was there. And then, of course, I had continued on it for 48 more miles. I could walk this morning, and walk without a limp, but there was definitely a pinching feeling, a sort of stiffness letting me know that I had tweaked something. I decided to take some time off and let it get back to feeling normal.

I had finished 238th out of 296 runners, 178th out of 207 runners in the men's division, 39th out of 43 in the men's 35- to 39-year-old division. Any way I looked at it, I was much closer to last place than first place. But I had finished a 50-mile race.

From 1992 to 2005, Jack Long Nissan in Longview, Texas, held a contest called "Hands on a Hardbody." The premise: Whoever could stand the longest next to a truck without taking their hand off it would drive it home. Contestants took one 5-minute break every hour and one 15-minute break every six hours. After 89 hours, Benny Perkins was the last person standing, and won the truck the first year of the contest, 1992.

In 1995, filmmakers S.R. Bindler and Kevin Morris followed the contest from beginning to end, interviewing current and past contestants. During the interviews from before the event that appear at the beginning of the documentary *Hands on a Hardbody*, almost all of the contestants are confident that they will not walk away until they've won the truck. They all have their stories and reasons—the truck will help them earn money, or they can't afford payments on a new car, or they believe that God wants them to win the truck. There is, of course, only one winner.

The filmmakers also interview an unnamed competitor in the 1993 contest, who said: "I'll never ever forget it, you know, it was just something that became a part of my life that I'll never forget. It was the best experience I ever had in my life." Then, remembering he's standing next to the person who won the contest that year and that he had gotten second place, he added, "Well, I can't say it was the best feeling. It was the second-best feeling. If I'd have won, it'd be the best feeling."

In the 1995 contest, the truck was valued at $15,000. The second-place prize was $250 cash, and the third-place prize was a gift certificate to Johnny Cace's Seafood and Steak House.

Near the end of the film, Benny Perkins, who placed third in the 1995 contest, speaks over footage of some of the more emotional moments of the competition:

"You basically learn the values of humanity," Perkins says. "Values that you would put on another human being, because you've seen other people struggling, fighting for the same thing you're fighting for. Wanting the same thing you're wanting. And you see them lose. That has value. Even losing. Because they at least tried. And there's not that many triers in the world today. There's not that many people that are willing to take a risk to do something. To stick themselves out in a position where they might get hurt. They don't want to do that. That's a risk. But yes, it teaches you human values. The very basic human values."

The world's longest footrace happens around a single city block around a school in Jamaica, Queens: The Sri Chinmoy Self-Transcendence 3100. The distance around the block is 0.5488 miles, so runners have to complete 5,649 laps of the block in order to complete the race. The time limit is 52 days, which requires an average of 59.62 miles of running each day. On paper, it sounds bananas, even if you have experience running ultramarathons. But when writer, ultrarunner, and teacher Devin Kelly made his way to the course to watch several times throughout the 2021 race, he saw something different. He wrote:

Another beauty of endurance is that it is happening at all times. It is everywhere we look. To see someone, anyone, in this world is to witness someone engaged in a feat of endurance. That's what struck me, each time I went out to Queens. How ordinary it felt to be there. How un-crazy the whole thing was.

One tragedy of living in this world is the way in which nearly any act—however trivial or radical—often becomes subsumed and consumed by the dominant narrative. Best intentions become exploited. Activists wind up competing for cash on a prime-time reality show. There can only be one winner. The very idea of limitlessness falls into this same trap. You witness someone breaking limits—running faster or farther than ever—and almost immediately such an act becomes a metaphor for the way in which we are supposed to approach our jobs, our lives, our loves. The trouble with this is that, when endurance is celebrated in this way, and pinned against what are seen as the daily failings of our lives, we collectively neglect to acknowledge the way in which simply being alive, and sometimes simply waking up—especially today, especially right now—is so often and for so many a feat of extraordinary endurance[15].

Bryce Carlson was no stranger to endurance events when he decided to run across the United States from Los Angeles to Washington, D.C., with a group of five other athletes in 2015. He'd run several ultramarathons, including six 100-mile races. But Race Across the USA, he thought, might be a research opportunity. He got in touch with Herman Pontzer, a professor of evolutionary anthropology at Duke University, and asked if Pontzer would like to follow the runners for the five-month run and measure their energy expenditure throughout.

Pontzer and a team of researchers had runners drink isotopically enriched water, enabling them to calculate the amount of carbon dioxide the runners' bodies produced every day, which gave the researchers the exact number of calories each athlete burned. Race Across the USA athletes ran one marathon a day, six days a week, for 15 to 20 weeks. Pontzer's team collected the data, plotted it over time, and compared it to previously collected metabolic data from other endurance activities: triathlons, 100-mile ultras, Antarctic expeditions, and the Tour de France.

All the events showed that after 20 days, energy expenditure leveled off, and flattened out at approximately 2.5 times the person's basal metabolic rate—the calories that person would burn while resting. After about 20 days of sustained activity (like running or cycling), the limit of human endurance is decided by the digestive tract. And everyone has that same metabolic limit: 2.5 times their basal metabolic rate. As Pontzer put it in an interview with *Duke Today*[16]: "There's just a limit to how many calories our guts can effectively absorb per day."

The team's study, published in the journal Science Advances[17], made headlines for a different reason, though: when they plotted the energy expenditure of carrying a baby to full term, something that had been measured in earlier studies, they found that pregnancy requires about the same level of energy as the endurance activities that we find to be so impressive.

"I don't think any woman who's gone through pregnancy is surprised by this," Pontzer told NPR[18]. "It's pushing your body to the very limits of what you can do. You know, it is the ultramarathon of human endurance, pregnancy. And it plots right on that same boundary of human capability with Tour de France cyclists and Arctic trekkers and everybody else."

The *New York Post* titled its story about the study: "Pregnant women are basically endurance athletes." CNN's headline[19]: "The two groups that reach the peak of human endurance? Extreme athletes and pregnant women."

100

In ultrarunning, the logical progression of races in the United States goes like this:

31 MILES (50 KM) → 50 MILES → 100 MILES

There are also plenty of 100-kilometer (62-mile) races, but 50-milers are much more common. So you could, after finishing a 50-miler, find a 100K to do, as a next step. But that didn't seem to be a common strategy, for whatever reason. Maybe the thinking was that 62 miles isn't that much farther than 50 miles, so 50 miles was just as good as 62? Or that the jump from 62 miles to 100 miles was so large (38 miles), that you might as well jump from 50 straight to 100?

When you're wrapped up in it, it seems to make a lot more sense. I thought of it this way: At home, if I sat down with a pint of ice cream and started eating it, if I got more than halfway through the pint, I'd start thinking, "Whoa, easy there, that's a lot of calories (and sugar)," and stop myself. But if I'm standing in line at the ice cream shop, I have no problem with a high school kid handing me a waffle cone with, let's be honest, a massive amount of ice cream in it, even though it's only a "single scoop." I would eat the whole thing, because that's "one serving." And if someone behind me ordered a waffle cone with two scoops, I would not think they were crazy. So I guess a 100-mile race is a metaphorical waffle cone with two scoops. Way too much for me, but still conceivable.

That said: I was not going to jump straight from 50 to 100 miles. I did not confidently breeze through my first 50-mile race, so I wanted to do at least one more 50-miler before I even started thinking about 100 miles.

For three weeks, I didn't run, and the pain in my foot gradually felt better and better. I didn't make time to see a doctor, since I was walking just fine, and I didn't think it felt painful enough that something was seriously wrong—it seemed like a perfectly normal physical response to making my body do something really abnormal.

When I started running three weeks later, my foot was no problem. What started becoming a problem over the summer was my IT band.

I was generally feeling pretty fit, but anytime I ran (or hiked, or ran and hiked) hilly trails, I'd get that pinching pain in the side of my left knee after about one and a half or two miles. I could stop and stretch it out, or alter my stride to make it less painful, but it was there, and it wasn't sustainable. If it popped up at eight miles, or 10 miles, there was no way I could go 50, let alone 100.

I tried all sorts of stretches. I tried the thing that everyone said would work: foam rolling. Foam rollers are self-torture devices for athletes. Essentially, you have a cylinder made of hard foam (or a plastic cylinder wrapped in hard foam broken into spiky or bumpy sections), and you drive it into a bit of soft tissue somewhere on your body in order to produce excruciating pain that you hope will make some other pain go away. For IT band issues, the general idea is that you lie down on your side, put the foam roller on the floor under your thigh, then put your hands down on the floor, lifting yourself up to put as much of your bodyweight as possible on the foam roller. Then you move back and forth, rolling your thigh up and down on the foam roller. Many people swear this "works," but it actually doesn't do shit.

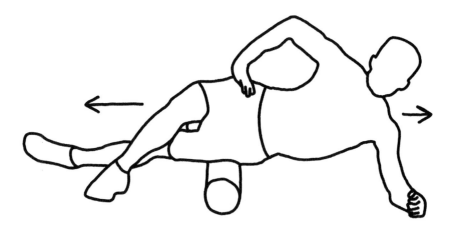

If you want to run and you have a nagging injury or pain, you essentially become an addict who has a problem that is obviously caused by the thing they're addicted to, and will search tirelessly for a solution, any solution, that will make their problem go away—except quitting the thing they're addicted to. Or maybe that's just me.

The summer I was training for my second 50-mile race and dealing with the IT band issue, I was also traveling around promoting a book I had written about my struggle with alcoholism, subsequent treatment and recovery, and eventual transition into rock climbing. I was not an expert at addiction and recovery, but I was starting to wonder if the one-day-at-a-time approach to sobriety was my first experience with endurance sports. At that point, I hadn't had a drink in 14 years, but the behavior and thinking patterns were still there:

Patient: Well, I've racked up quite a bit of debt, really screwed up some relationships, and I've gotten arrested a few times, and now I'm in some legal trouble.

Doctor: Says here you've been getting blackout drunk a few times a week for several years—think that might have something to do with all of that?

Patient: I mean ... I don't know ... maybe? I'm not sure. Seems like it might just be bad luck.

Patient: Yeah, it's a pain, right here, in the side of my knee. Starts up after I've run a few miles, or run up and down a few hills.

Doctor: Says here you've been running about 40 miles a week, and you're competing in ultramarathons. Maybe you should take a break from running?

Patient: OK, I guess I could see how you'd come to that conclusion. But what else could I do, besides taking a break from running?

What eventually worked:

When I ran downhill, I turned my left foot slightly outward, which put more of my weight onto my hip and glute. I realized I had an incredibly weak left glute and quad—I could do one-legged squats on my right leg just fine, but they were almost impossible to do on my left side. I started doing exercises to strengthen my left leg and hip, and my IT band pain went away. The foam roller started to gather dust.

Partway through the third lap of the Bear Chase Trail Race 50-Mile, around Mile 35, I decided to quit. I was nearing the end of my third 12.5-mile lap, with one lap to go. I didn't have any injuries—I just didn't have it in me to finish. I had excuses ready: I had been traveling for work for a couple weeks, and had gotten off a plane at 7 p.m. the night before, gotten home at 8:00, and the 6:30 a.m. race start time came early. I was tired.

Jayson and I had started the race and run the first two and a half laps together, chatting away. He had entered the 100K, so he'd have one extra lap after I finished the 50-mile race (if I finished). Around Mile 30 or so, I noticed he was going a little bit faster than me, and I was struggling to keep up. He looked back, I yelled "Just go," and we parted ways. A few miles later, my morale had dipped to just above zero. I slowed down to a sad shuffle, and practiced what I would say to Hilary when I got to the start/finish area at the end of my third lap. She would understand.

Hilary and I had been together for four years. When we met, I was living in a 2005 Chevy Astrovan, which was not a nice van, but it had all-wheel drive and only cost $6500 when I bought it from a place called Johnny's Auto Sales and Pawn in Denver. She was working as a legal assistant in a law office, which she had transitioned to from her job as a waitress at a nearby vegetarian restaurant, where the lawyer she worked for was a regular. And when I was in town, I was a regular there too.

After a whirlwind four dates in a week and a half, I had left Denver for some traveling, and then bounced in and out of the city in my van for the rest of the year. I was barely making it as a full-time adventure writer when I got a contract from an apparel company to do some writing and editing work for them—work that I figured Hilary and I could split, if she quit her job at the law office and moved into the van with me. She had a journalism degree, but hadn't been using it for the past few years after getting laid off from an associate editor job at a trade magazine.

She moved into the van with me after only six months of dating. I taught her how to rock climb, she taught me how to mountain bike, and we bounced around the West for a year and a half in the van, working on our laptops in coffee shops and libraries, making just enough money to scrape by and afford a cheap hotel room where we could take a shower and regroup every once in a while. She got her writing career started again, this time as an essayist who took her experiences in the mountains and found deeper meaning behind them, beyond the pursuit of beautiful scenery and adrenaline.

Hilary could move in the mountains, carry a heavy backpack, was kind, and had a tough streak buried underneath her generally calm and thoughtful presence. Where I was always looking to the next thing, or to improve on something, she was present, grateful, and happy. Out of the two of us, she was the one who actually enjoyed running for the running, not as a self-flagellating avenue used to arrive at the real reason. She ran because, for her, it was fun. I ran for the exact opposite reason—because it was not fun.

As I jogged into the start/finish area, the clock was ticking through the 7-hour 49-minute mark into 7:50. After finishing my first two laps in 2:24 and 2:30, my third lap had taken me 2 hours and 56 minutes, and I wasn't feeling anything like a second wind coming on for a final lap. I was finished. You can't win 'em all. Sometimes you eat the bear, sometimes the bear eats you. Hilary walked up to meet me. She was fully dressed to run, her vest cinched up, water bottles filled, pacer bib pinned to her shirt.

Now I felt guilty. She was ready to go. Excited, even, after sitting around for almost eight hours. How was I going to break the news to her?

In the end, I could not muster the strength to quit. She asked how I was feeling.

"Not great," I mumbled. "I don't feel like finishing."

"OK," she said.

"But ..." I said, "You look like you would like to go for a run."

"Yeah, I would like to get some exercise," she said.

"OK, but I think I am going to be doing a lot of walking on the last lap."

"Sure."

I filled up my water bottles, got some snacks, and begrudgingly hiked out of the start/finish area to start the final 12.5-mile lap.

It took us 3 hours and 27 minutes, a full hour longer than my first lap. We averaged almost 17 minutes per mile. But I finished another 50-mile race, and a little bit faster this time, for whatever that was worth.

Almost exactly two hours later, Jayson came flying through the finish line in high spirits, in ninth place in the 100K race. He looked at least 10 times better than I had felt when I crossed the 50-mile finish. I was happy for him, and happy for me, because we could all leave and go get some pizza.

In *Born to Run*, Christopher McDougall makes the case that human beings have running in our DNA, and for proof, we can look at the ancient practice of persistence hunting. To grossly oversimplify the concept: a group of human beings separate one large animal from its pack, and chase it, and because of our ability to run long distances at a moderate pace, the humans could pursue the animal until it eventually ran itself to death.

Nowadays, hunting is largely optional for most of the population in a country like the United States, and when we do hunt, it's with rifles or bows, not with running an off-road ultramarathon with eight of our friends while chasing an antelope. I've personally never persistence hunted. Like a lot of people who do cardiovascular exercise in the 21st century, part of the reason I do it is to burn "extra" calories so they don't turn into extra body mass. Extra body mass, in large enough amounts of excess over a long enough period of time, being something that could cause major health problems and potentially an early death.

Sometimes running will come up in a conversation I'm having with someone who is not a runner, and they will say something like "I don't run unless someone's chasing me." I acknowledge that this is a sane way to live one's life, and definitely closer to what is considered normal behavior. The logic there is that we've escaped the food chain, large predators are not pursuing us, and therefore there is no reason to run. This is sound logic.

If you thought about the persistence hunting in our not-so-distant past, you might say that marathon runners and ultramarathon runners are just simulating hunting, but now we're doing it because we're eating too much food, not because we need to acquire more food. We're just imitating hunting, or imitating being chased by a predator, and isn't that ridiculous? If we brought one of our persistence hunting ancestors to an ultramarathon starting line, they'd probably be quite confused that we were all lined up to chase nothing but our own dreams, and sense of meaning.

Ancestor: So there is no lion chasing you?

Ultramarathon runner: Nope.

Ancestor: And all of you runners are not chasing an antelope?

Ultramarathon runner: Nope, just running.

Ancestor: It's like you're hunting, but not really hunting.

Ultramarathon runner: Yep.

Ancestor: And you find meaning in this simulation of something that was, for us, essential for survival?

Ultramarathon runner: Yeah.

Ancestor: The future is weird.

Ultramarathon runner: Wait till I tell you about football, which is our war simulation sport, and, um, pornography.

The month after the Bear Chase 50-mile race, I got a cold. I was traveling all the time for work, not resting, and eventually the cold turned into a sinus infection, which lasted for weeks. On a flight to Phoenix, one of my ears plugged up with fluid, and didn't pop on the descent, so I spent a week with all the sounds coming in that ear muffled like my head was underwater. I ran four times the entire month of October, 23 miles total, and twice in November, eight miles total.

Jayson and I kept talking about the idea of a 100-mile race, when we should do it, which one we should do, how long we'd need to get ready, whether or not we could actually ever be ready. I assumed my cold/sinus infection would not last forever.

We decided we wanted:

- a race somewhere in the mountains in the western U.S.

- enough ups and downs to be really challenging

- maybe close to home in Colorado

- a cutoff time that was doable for us

- a race with a known reputation

- but not a race that was so famous that it was impossible to get into

- and a race that we were qualified for already, so we wouldn't have to run some other race in order to get in

At 5:50 a.m. on January 7, my phone alarm went off, and I sat up on the sleeper sofa at my friends' house in Seattle, opened my laptop, and signed up for the 2017 Run Rabbit Run 100 in Steamboat Springs, Colorado. It was 102.9 miles, 20,391 feet of elevation gain, hitting a high point of 10,557 feet. It cost $295 to register. The elevation profile looked like this:

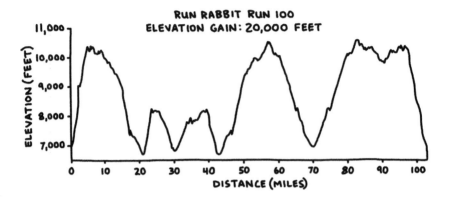

In ultramarathon races with aid stations every five or eight miles, you could arguably run carrying very minimal gear—maybe just a single water bottle strapped to your hand, and a couple gels in small pockets in your shorts. You could refill your bottle at every aid station, eat the food supplied by the race, and if you did it correctly, you'd be in no danger of dying of dehydration or starvation. Lots of fast runners do this. Of course, they're not out on the race course nearly as long as the rest of us mere mortals.

In a marathon, the winners cross the finish line in a little more than two hours, or two and a half hours. The average time of other runners is closer to four hours, or four and a half. In a 50-mile ultramarathon, for example, the 2016 Ice Age Trail 50-Mile race, the winner crossed the finish line in 6 hours, 36 minutes and 45 seconds, almost five hours before Jayson and I shuffled in. In longer races such as the Ultra Trail du Mont Blanc (Football: World Cup; Ultrarunning: Ultra Trail du Mont Blanc), the gap widens significantly, with winners finishing around 21 or 22 hours, and the final runners crossing the finish around the 46-hour mark. Which is an entire 24-hour day, in which those people burn several thousand calories.

So running vests are popular, especially in longer races—in mountain 100-milers, it's fairly uncommon to see anyone, fast or not-as-fast, not wearing a vest. Some races even require runners to carry minimum safety gear like water bottles, headlamps, and emergency blankets.

Of course, when you're training for an ultramarathon, there are no magical volunteers standing out in the woods to fill your water bottles, or hand you Oreos, or ask you how you're feeling. So you pack all your supplies in a vest.

Running vests range from the minimalist, with two pockets that each hold one water bottle and one or two additional pockets for a few gels or other snacks, to the more elaborate mountain vests, which have several additional large pockets for extra clothing and supplies, as well as bungee cords to cinch extra items to the outside, and/or attachment points to hold folded-up trekking poles.

A 17-ounce soft water bottle, when filled with water, weighs about one pound, so running with two full water bottles strapped to your chest can change your running form a little bit (not to mention if you have an extra full bottle or two in the back of your vest). Everything else you take to run can be space-age and ultralight (maybe you buy the five-ounce rain jacket instead of the eight-ounce one), but there's no way of making water weigh less.

Here is a drawing of my vest:

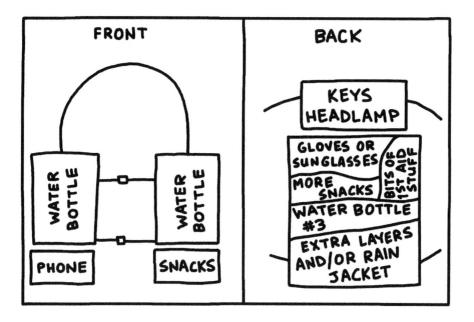

As a kid, like most kids, I imagine, I hated walking anywhere more than a few blocks, even if there was ice cream at the end of that walk. And when you're years away from getting a driver's license, obtaining a bicycle and learning how to ride it is pretty much a superpower. You can make skid marks in a parking lot somewhere, jump it off things, experiment with accidental soft-tissue damage, and—very important to young kids whose brains are still forming and who don't have a grasp on things like consequences for their actions—you can find the biggest hill around and see how fast you can get going down it. But best of all: You can leave your neighborhood. You can ride to baseball practice, or to the swimming pool, or to a convenience store to buy candy. Your map of the world expands. My running vest opened up terrain in the same way my first bicycle, a Huffy Thunder 50, did when I was a kid.

My running vest, fully loaded with four 17-ounce water bottles and about 1,000 calories of gels, blocks, and waffles, could keep me moving for four hours or more without stopping, even on a hot Colorado summer day. On a really good day, I could cover 15 or 18 miles in that amount of time. Mostly, though, Jayson and I trained in shorter loops, circling back to a trailhead parking lot to refill food and water and reapply sunscreen from the back of our car. Jayson's Subaru Forester was our aid station, unstaffed, usually sitting out in the direct sunlight.

Here is a drawing of the back of Jayson's car:

The first week of February, we started training for the Run Rabbit Run 100 in earnest, powered mostly by the anxiety of not knowing what we were doing, but fully knowing that the race we had signed up for offered huge potential for failure. The Run Rabbit Run 100 doesn't bill itself as the toughest race in North America, or the toughest race anywhere, or anything like that. It's just a 100-mile trail race, in the mountains. But out of the 250 or 300 people who sign up each year, one in three don't finish. This information was available on the internet, so we knew it.

Once we started training for it, we tried everything. We drank smoothies with raw turmeric root in them to combat inflammation, as well as tart cherry juice. Jayson wore compression socks, and brought recovery drinks to our long runs to drink immediately after. As soon as I got home from our long runs, I'd stick my feet and lower legs in a five-gallon bucket of ice water. I gave up coffee for three months before the race, thinking it would keep me from getting dehydrated.

We followed a mileage plan as closely as we could, running on our own during the week and then meeting up on Saturdays and Sundays for our weekly "long run" in the foothills, or sometimes two back-to-back longer runs. One week, we'd do a 20-mile run, stopping back at the car once or twice to refill food and water, and the next week, we'd meet up for a 16-mile run on Saturday and a 14-mile run on Sunday. We kept increasing the distance of our long runs, doing a 31-mile run one weekend, then a 22-miler and 20-miler run on back-to-back days another weekend.

Some days, I felt like I was getting stronger, but mostly, I felt like I was aging at a rapid pace. Pain came and went, popping up in one part of a leg or foot during a run, sticking around throughout the day, and then disappearing one or two days later, only to be replaced by a different pain somewhere else. Every single one of them was a threat to our 100-mile race—I never knew when something would hurt, then get worse, then turn into an injury that would derail my whole summer.

That's the way I felt, anyway.

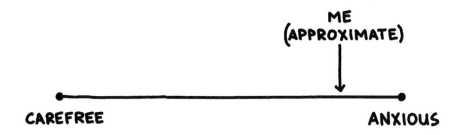

Another way to look at it might have been: Wow, what a lucky person I am, to be able to run 15 or 20 miles in one go, on trails a half-hour from my apartment, with a dear friend who shares my goals and never runs out of conversation topics. If something goes wrong, I'll just deal with it.

After logging hundreds of miles on rocky trails without so much as spraining an ankle or smashing a toenail, with a couple months till the Run Rabbit Run 100, I slipped in the shower at home, crashing through the shower curtain and onto the floor. It would have made for a funny movie scene, except for the fact that I ripped a hole in my abdominal wall. Or more accurately, I enlarged a hole in my abdominal wall.

When I was 14, in eighth grade, I got really into weightlifting, and somehow during a deadlift or something like that, I managed to tear a small hole in my abdominal wall, directly above my belly button. I went to the doctor to have it checked out, and the doctor said, *Yes, it's a small hernia. As long as it doesn't get worse, you might as well leave it be—it's more trouble than it's worth at this point to fix it surgically.* Every once in a great while, a tiny bit of my intestine would pop out, and then it would go back in. No big deal.

For 24 years, it didn't get worse. Then I fell out of the shower and it definitely got fucking worse. It was bigger, for sure. When I changed positions to stand up or sit down, I felt pain that let me know that part of my intestine was essentially leaking out of my insides. Using my index and middle finger, I would gently push my intestine back through the hole, and start worrying about it. Then I'd research it on the internet, think about trying to get it fixed, realize that surgery would basically mean I couldn't run our 100-mile race, so then I'd go back to work and try to ignore it.

The hole in my abdominal wall didn't hurt when I ran. That was the one optimistic data point. So I kept running, carrying in the back of my head a little worry about a ping pong ball-sized hole where there shouldn't be a hole. My mother, a nurse practitioner, told me as long as I was not shitting blood, I was probably OK. I think she may have used more appropriate medical terminology when she said it.

Finally, sick of the anxiety about it, I took five consecutive days off of running, the longest stretch of rest I'd had since January. On the sixth day, the hernia seemed back to normal, or at least smaller than it had been. I allowed myself a half-sigh of partial relief and went back to work, running and hiking 16 miles on Saturday and 10 miles on Sunday.

The next weekend, with a month to go before the race, we scheduled our longest run, which we figured should be between 50 and 62 miles, and about 10,000 feet of elevation gain—or exactly half of the elevation gain of the Run Rabbit Run 100. I had lobbied to do our big run a little higher in the mountains than normal, at Golden Gate Canyon State Park, for hopefully cooler early August temperatures, some shade in a more forested area, and also to put us at a little bit higher altitude, since we'd be up a little higher during our race.

We parked Jayson's car at a trailhead, elevation 8,200 feet, cinched up our vests, and started doing 12.5-mile laps just after 8:30 a.m.

Each lap would involve three main climbs: 900 feet in the first two miles out of the parking lot, a mile and a half climbing 630 feet, and a two-mile section later that climbed about 420 feet before four miles of mostly downhill running back to the trailhead to complete the loop and grab some more water and food before heading out again to do another loop.

As an approximation of half of the Run Rabbit Run, it was the best idea we could come up with: all singletrack trails with plenty of rocks and roots, similar elevation, and 50 miles. We didn't quite hit 10,000 feet of ascent—just 9,400—but by the time we finished our fourth lap, it was 8:57 p.m., and we'd been moving nonstop for a little over 12 hours, save for our three stops back at the car/aid station. Would one more lap be that much more helpful in our training? We decided it wouldn't—or at least it wouldn't be helpful enough to justify staying out until past midnight.

In a 2014 study published in the British Journal of Sports Medicine[20], researchers surveyed 2,794 runners competing in the 2013 Ultra-Trail du Mont-Blanc, the 2013 Leadville Trail 100, and the 2013 Western States Endurance Run, to determine why people fail to finish ultramarathon races. The most common factors:

- inability to make the cut off time (23.1%)

- nausea and/or vomiting (16.5%)

- injury during the race (16.5%)

- an ongoing injury (13.3%).

Basically an exact list of the things that cycled through my mind every day in the six months leading up to the Run Rabbit Run 100.

If I looked at our training, nutrition, and self-care throughout the year, it seemed like we were doing a pretty good job. But there was no way around it: Neither of us had ever run 100 miles before, and nothing we could do or learn before our race was going to make us sleep easier. There was no training run, bit of internet data, or wisdom that would enable me to confidently say, "Oh yeah, we're going to be just fine, no problem."

It didn't help that both of us tended toward the anxious end of the spectrum: We were both insomniacs. I'd had heart palpitations before, in advance of a big event. Jayson couldn't drink coffee, or even eat chocolate after 3 p.m., or he'd toss and turn all night. So our individual worries about the race spiraled around each other, forming a double helix of stress.

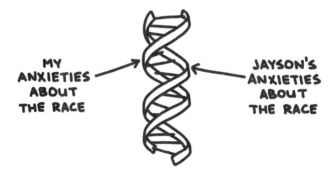

MY ANXIETIES ABOUT THE RACE   JAYSON'S ANXIETIES ABOUT THE RACE

Still, nobody ever mentioned the one thing that would 100 percent without a doubt settle our minds, which was: not doing the race.

One of the most famous Robert Frost quotes people use for motivational purposes is often re-phrased as "The only way out is through." In Frost's original poem, "A Servant to Servants," it's actually written "I can see no way out but through." That's how I felt about running a 100-mile race. But obviously, going through the Run Rabbit Run was not the only way out. Quitting was always on the table. So was starting the race and not finishing, which I guess is another version of quitting. In almost every version of physical exercise we do as human beings, quitting is always an option. You can literally say, "Yeah, I don't want to do this anymore."

You can go out on a run one day, telling yourself you have to run six miles, and you can quit after three miles. You can run five miles, realize you're not having fun, and quit running for the rest of your life. You can quit before you even get out the door. You can be ready to go in your running clothes, lacing up your shoes, and decide you'd rather not run today, and grab a bag of chips and sit on your couch and watch Netflix or read a book. You can do this while wearing your running clothes.

No one was going to die if we didn't do the Run Rabbit Run. It's not like we were carrying a human heart across a mountain pass for a transplant surgery for the Dalai Lama, or carrying a cease-fire agreement that would end a decades-long war hours before one side launched a nuclear missile. We were just two idiots, trying to do a hard thing, along with a couple hundred other idiots.

Well, everybody does something, usually anyway.

In the 1950s, the British and French governments began to research supersonic transport, in hopes of developing a commercial aircraft that could transport airline passengers faster than the speed of sound, or about 740 mph. (Modern commercial airline flights usually operate at speeds between 460 and 575 mph.) The plane, with its ogival delta design, looked futuristic, and would make it possible for civilians—albeit wealthy civilians—to fly at speeds that only military pilots had experienced. A Concorde flight from Paris to New York would take half as long: three and a half hours, compared to eight hours in a commercial airliner. By the mid-1960s, the project was headed toward reality, and major airlines placed orders for more than 100 Concordes.

Here is an overhead view of the Concorde's ogival delta design:

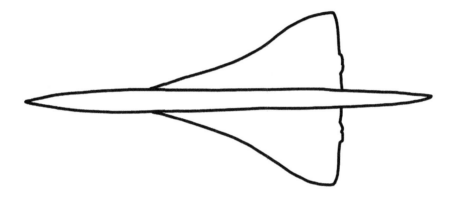

The first commercial Concorde flights began running in 1976, but by then, the prospects had shrunk. Because of the skyrocketing costs of the development of the plane, the 1973 oil crisis, the 1973-1974 stock market crash, and a ban on Concordes landing at JFK airport because of concerns about the sonic boom the plane produced, many airlines canceled their Concorde orders, and only 20 of the aircraft were ever produced, and only 14 of those were actually used by commercial airlines: British Airways and Air France, who used them on two routes. The average cost of a ticket on a supersonic flight was $12,000.

By the early 1980s, the Concorde's future had dimmed significantly, and the final Concorde flight took place in October 2003. The French and British governments continued to pour money into the plane's development for years, long after the idea of financial success became a lost cause. This is why the economic idea known as the "sunk cost fallacy" is sometimes called the Concorde fallacy: a company continues to invest in something because they've already put so much money into it, not because it will actually pay off. If you've ever justified sitting through an awful movie in a theater because you paid 12 bucks for the ticket, or decided to pay for an expensive repair on a car because you've already spent a ton of money repairing the car, you have personal experience with the sunk cost fallacy.

We ran more than 1,200 miles in the six months leading up to our 100-mile race, which, on paper, seemed like a smart investment in research and development. In the final weeks leading up to the race, though, I did not feel strong, or fit, or ready. I felt creaky, worn-down, and like something in one of my feet or legs could just explode at any time.

On July 25, 2000, after the Concorde's near-perfect safety record for the previous 24 years, Air France Flight 4590 crashed just after taking off from Charles De Gaulle Airport, killing all 100 passengers and nine crew members on the plane.

You can run a 100-mile race by yourself, without inviting any friends and family to join you before or after the race, or meet you somewhere along the race course to provide food, supplies, and encouragement. People do it. We did not do that. We invited Jayson's girlfriend, Kate, and my girlfriend, Hilary, as well as my parents, our friends Syd and Debi, and a couple other friends to pace us for the last 33 miles of the race, and also to shoot some video footage for a film project. Having more friends there, we thought, would make it more fun, more like a little party.

Some race courses make it easy to rendezvous with friends and family. The Javelina Jundred, a 100-mile and 100K race near Phoenix, takes place on one big loop that's approximately 20 miles. There are three aid stations on the loop, but besides the start/finish area where each loop begins and ends, runners' crews (friends and family) are not able to see the runner on the course. So if you come to support your spouse, friend, or co-worker during the Javelina Jundred 100-miler, you just hang out and wait for them to finish each loop. Maybe you go into the city and have a meal, or do some shopping in between, but the logistics are simple: You stay put, they come to you, you help them with whatever they need whenever they come through every two and a half to six hours, and they take off again.

The Run Rabbit Run, like many races, was a bit more complicated. The race was one big loop that crosses over itself in a couple different spots. The map looked like this:

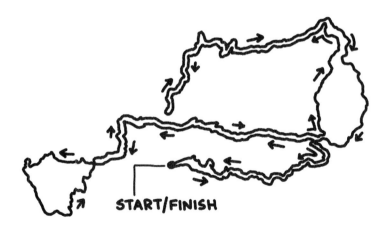

START/FINISH

The race had had three big climbs of more than 3,000 vertical feet and two smaller climbs around 1,500 feet each:

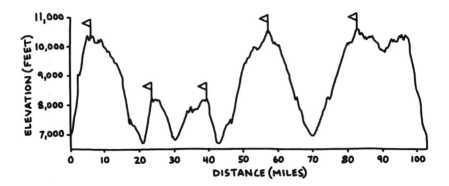

Crews were only allowed to meet their runners at the aid stations at these mile markers:

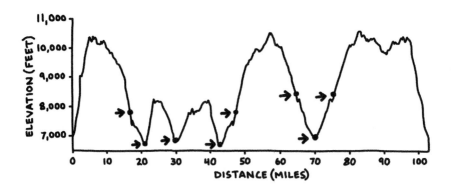

But some of those aid stations were more complicated to get to than others, so we decided that our crew would meet us at these three spots, so we'd see them at the start, at 21.3 miles, at 29.9 miles, at 42.1 miles, at 65.3 miles, at 74.3 miles, and then at the finish line.

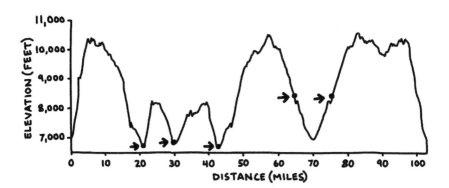

Which seems like a decent plan, but when you start doing the math it gets a little complicated. We knew we could, in theory, run Miles 1-50 in about 12-ish hours, but that definitely didn't mean we could run miles 51-102.9 in 12 hours. We sat down and tried to do the math to estimate roughly when we'd come through each aid station, but there was just no getting around the fact that we had no idea what we were doing, or what would happen. What if it was really hot during the day and we got dehydrated? What if we started too fast and blew up halfway through? What if we had issues with the altitude? If we ran a reasonable first 50 miles and got through them in 13 or 14 hours, would the second 50 take 15 or 16 hours? Or 18 hours?

So predicting when we would get to the aid station at Mile 65 was a bit difficult. And it wasn't like we had cell phone reception and could just call ahead like hey, we'll be there in about 45 minutes, maybe you could grab a couple pizzas from Domino's, drive down to the shuttle bus parking at Olympian Hall, get on the shuttle bus for 30 minutes, and meet us at the Dry Lake aid station. At 2:30 a.m.

I stood at the end of the bed at our rental condo, looking at two 10-liter stuff sacks, trying to be sensible. If I let my anxious thoughts pack my drop bags, I would need two suitcases. I reminded myself that I really only needed some necessities, as the bags would be sitting at aid stations, where volunteers would have food and first aid supplies. I needed a pair of running pants, a little food, maybe some extra clothes.

In longer races, runners get to use drop bags, or a bag of their stuff that's transported to a certain aid station. You can put whatever you want in your drop bag, and most races just have a maximum size limit. Drop bags are helpful to runners who don't have friends meeting them along the course, or have dietary restrictions, or want extra socks or shoes to change into (after a wet section of the race or before a steep section, etc.), or extra clothes for changing temperatures. Runners give their drop bags to race staff before the race, and the bags are ferried to the proper locations to wait for runners to arrive. After the race is over, staff members bring all the drop bags to a pickup location. In the Run Rabbit Run, drop bags were allowed at a few spots along the course.

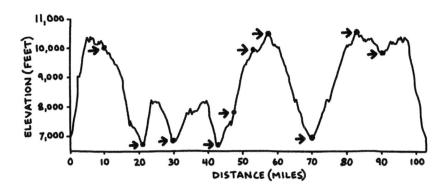

One of my drop bags would have some food and extra clothes at the 57.7-mile/81.9-mile aid station. If things were going OK, we'd get there between 8:00 and 10:00 p.m., just as the temperature was starting to drop. This was also the highest point of the race, at 10,557 feet, where the temperature could potentially be colder. So we filled up one dry bag each with running pants, light gloves, a few other layers, an extra pair of socks, and some foods we liked. We figured we'd put the pants on at Mile 57.7 for the cold hours, then drop them when the sun rose, either with our crew at Mile 69.8, or back at the drop bag at mile 81.9. We put some food, sunscreen, wet wipes, and extra socks in a second drop bag, at the 11.2/52.2/90.1-mile mark, just in case.

Runners often say "running is so simple," because the only special gear you need to do it is a pair of running shoes. The few people who run barefoot would say you don't even need that. It's true: For a six-mile run starting and ending at my house in decent weather, I usually just put on shoes, socks, shorts, and a t-shirt, and go. It's so simple.

To run, and train for, a 100-mile race, I had acquired and used:

- A pair of shoes for running on roads

- A pair of shoes for running on trails

- A second pair of shoes for running on trails, to serve as a backup during the Run Rabbit Run

- My running vest

- Multiple pairs of shorts made of quick-drying synthetic fabrics

- Multiple T-shirts made of quick-drying synthetic fabrics

- A lightweight hooded jacket to wear if it was cold and windy

- A lightweight hooded jacket to wear if it was raining

- A pair of lightweight gloves

- A lightweight beanie

- A packable baseball cap with mesh vents and a soft visor

- Several pairs of running socks

- A pair of fabric sun sleeves to shield my arms from UV rays

- A fancy GPS watch to track my mileage and elevation gain

- Dozens of packages of CLIF BLOKS (essentially higher-tech gummy bears) and dozens of Honey Stinger waffles (essentially higher-tech stroopwafels)

- Four soft-sided water bottles that fit in my running vest

- Several sticks of Body Glide, a lubricant to prevent chafing

- Several tubes of sunscreen

- A pair of lightweight trekking poles

There is a saying in the bicycling world, and also in the skiing world, that the number of bikes (or skis) you need is N + 1, and N = the number of bikes/skis you currently own. This is a half-joke about the tendency to want a new thing even though you have a perfectly good, very similar thing, at home already. Bicycle manufacturers offer road bikes, commuter bikes, mountain bikes, downhill mountain bikes, gravel bikes, touring bikes, fat bikes (for riding on snow, but also for riding wherever you want), cargo bikes, folding bikes, cruiser bikes, tandem bikes, and others. If you're a skier, you can talk yourself into buying a similar variety of skis if you want to. On a much less expensive level, you can do the same thing with coffee mugs, or kitchen gadgets, or shoes.

Ultrarunning is not simple, compared with running shorter distances. But it is probably cheaper than buying lots of pairs of skis, or N + 1 bicycles.

Another saying, in the backpacking world: You pack your fears. Meaning, you try to mentally catalogue everything that can go wrong, and prepare for it by bringing everything you can think of that might help you deal with it. This type of thinking can result in a pretty heavy backpack. The converse of that is the saying "The more you know, the less you need," which is when you have experience, knowledge, and confidence, and don't feel the need to pack, say, a second water filter just in case your water filter fails. Gradually, your packing gets simpler, and your pack gets lighter.

We packed way more food, clothes, and medical supplies than we needed into our drop bags, and packed nine friends into a condo for our race, and even with all of that, I was still scared.

The day before the start of the race, we went to a big tent behind the Grand Hotel at the bottom of Steamboat Ski Resort to pick up our race packets, including our bibs, and to hand off our drop bags. At the pre-race meeting, Fred Abramowitz, the race director, got up in front of all the runners and grabbed a microphone to give us some updates and a bit of a pep talk. Some bullet points from his talk:

- 100 miles is really far

- It's harder than you think it is, and it's going to hurt more than you think it will

- There's a forest fire nearby, and it's affecting the air quality, but in general, if you don't already have respiratory issues, you will probably be fine

- Most people will be running Miles 21 through 41 in the afternoon sun, and it's going to be pretty hot

We tried to remain cautiously optimistic. We drank lots of water, tried to rest, and snacked nervously. I laid out the shorts, shirt, wind jacket, socks, and hat I'd wear to start the race, packed a backpack of stuff for Hilary to bring to the aid stations where we'd meet them, packed a bag of food for Syd to bring, and stuffed my vest with everything I thought I'd need in the first 29 miles of the race.

I wanted to sleep, but I knew it was going to be almost impossible to relax, no matter what. I just wanted to fast-forward to 8:00 a.m. and start the race. I took a melatonin and managed to get a few hours of good sleep before my alarm went off and I shuffled into the kitchen to make some oatmeal and start drinking water.

After eight months of alternately looking forward to and dreading this race, jogging through the starting line arch and finally making the first few steps of actual progress toward finishing would be an absolute relief.

In 2003, neuroscientist Sonia Cavigelli and psychologist Martha McClintock conducted a study to investigate their hypothesis that people who have a fear of novelty, or a "fearful behavioral style emerging early in life," would have increased adrenal activation, and because of that, die earlier. Essentially, responding to new things with fear and stress shortens your life.

They studied Norway rats, who have about a two-year lifespan in the wild. They established that they could classify rats as neophobic (hesitant to explore a novel environment) or neophilic (willing to explore a novel environment), based on behavioral differences, and that the behavior differences started in the rats' infancy—they were "shy" or "bold" from a very young age. To do this, they placed each rat in a large (to a rat) arena, about four feet by four feet, and watched how the rat reacted to being in a new environment with a new object in the arena each time. Shy rats would move along the walls, and bold rats would check out the novel object.

The rats were tested every six months, and the shy rats stayed shy, and the bold rats stayed bold. The bold rats' stress hormones would go back to normal more quickly than those in the shy rats, and in the end, the bold rats lived 20 percent longer than the shy rats.

Dr. Kelly Lambert covered this study in her classes, and in her book, *The Lab Rat Chronicles*, where she wrote: "Of course, this bold response may not be as healthy in the real world; I often tell my students that the bold rat probably would have died in a motorcycle accident in the outside world. All things being equal, however, you're better off boldly going where no rat has gone before." [21]

Two hundred and forty-two runners in all sorts of brightly-colored outfits milled around the starting line in the morning sun, maybe excited, maybe nervous, maybe overjoyed, maybe terrified, maybe all of those things together. I felt somewhere between nervous and numb, or at least calm. With 20 minutes to go until the race start, we were finally at a point where we couldn't do anything else to prepare—there was no more time to train, to sleep, to plan, or really even worry. At this point, beyond eating a banana or stretching, we were as ready as we were going to get.

The Run Rabbit Run field was split into two categories: Tortoises and Hares, Hares being the faster group, including the professional runners, who competed for the race's fairly large prize money. When we registered for the race, we had to register as Tortoises or Hares, and I didn't even read the guidelines for the Hare division—I just checked the Tortoise box. The Tortoises, all 242 of us, started at 8:00 a.m. The 72 runners in the Hare division started four hours later, at noon, meaning a good chunk of them would pass us on the race course at some point.

Jayson and I hadn't talked at all about where we should try to line up at the start. Towards the front, middle, or back? We went to the back.

The race course ran for a few hundred feet along the base of the Steamboat Ski Resort, under the gondola, and immediately turned left to go straight uphill. Running through the arch at the start, which we of course did, is almost comically aspirational, because a few hundred steps later, literally everyone stopped running and started hiking uphill. The race had 20,000 feet of elevation gain, and 3,500 feet of that was in the first 4.4 miles. We were hiking straight up grassy slopes that people would pay money to ski down three months later. First a green ski run called Stampede, then up a blue run called Heavenly Daze, and then service roads to a spot on the shoulder of Mt. Werner, at 10,370 feet.

We hiked for two and a half hours to reach the 4.4-mile mark at the first aid station.

We felt pretty good at the first aid station, as we grabbed a handful of potato chips and waffles almost without breaking stride, and started to run on the rolling singletrack through the forest. We felt fine at the next aid station at 10.8 miles, too. We were in 198th place at that point, at 3 hours and 26 minutes. The course started going downhill, on singletrack that gradually became more rocky and technical as it dropped back toward the town of Steamboat Springs, finally hitting a road, where we jogged on mellow downhill asphalt for four miles into town to another aid station, where we'd see our friends.

We entered the mid-day part of our race, the temperature climbed, and we left the 21.3-mile aid station to start hiking uphill, for a 1,400-foot climb in full sun. Partway up, I started not feeling so good. I was mildly nauseous, and said so to Jayson, and he said he was too. We stopped talking to each other and kept hiking uphill. A longtime ultrarunner, Vivian, had messaged me a few days before the race with a piece of advice for my first 100-mile race: "If you feel good, slow down. If you feel bad, eat something." So I ate something.

We eventually went down, saw our friends at the 30-mile aid station, and started heading back up again, a gradual 1,400-foot climb. The sun started to dip, and the fast runners, the Hares, started to pass us. As they approached from behind, they'd say something along the lines of "good job" or "nice work," which was part encouragement, but partly, "excuse me," as they blew past us. They ran up hills we were walking, or in the case of one very fast runner in baggy shorts, Courtney Dauwalter, they bounded down an incline we had decided was steep enough to walk. She would win the women's Hare division, crossing the finish line at about 8:40 a.m. the next morning.

Around this time, I started noticing that we had passed one guy a few times, leapfrogging him, probably because we took so long at aid stations and I assume he breezed right through. He was shirtless, hiking alone, carrying a single water bottle. He looked to be in his mid-50s. It seemed like everyone was wearing some sort of vest or pack to carry water, food, and other supplies, except this guy, cruising along with a single bottle, like he'd just parked at the trailhead and was out for a five-mile day hike.

Later, at an aid station, Jayson heard a volunteer skeptically comment on the man's lack of gear, and another volunteer assured them that oh no, he knows what he's doing—he'd finished dozens of ultramarathons and several 100-milers before.

As the course headed downhill toward the aid station at Mile 42, we stopped to check on a runner sitting on the side of the trail, who looked like the heat was getting the best of him. He said he was OK, so we kept moving. A minute later, we saw another racer headed the wrong way a couple hundred feet down a different trail and I yelled to get his attention. He turned around and started back uphill toward us, saying thanks for the heads-up.

The sun finally disappeared and we clicked on our headlamps for the last mile to the aid station. As we jogged, it started to sink in for me: It was dark and we weren't even halfway through. We were still ahead of about 80 runners, but my hope of finishing in under 30 hours was starting to fade. I sat down in a camp chair to change my socks, and Hilary brought over a plate of pancakes and eggs. Jayson and I stuffed our vests with warm layers, as the temperature would start dropping and continue to get colder for the next 11 hours, until 6:30 the next morning. Our pants were in our drop bags at the Long Lake aid station at 9,900 feet, 10 miles and 2,900 feet uphill from where we sat. So we started going uphill in the dark, to get our pants.

A little after midnight, we reached the Long Lake aid station at Mile 52, to find runners in various states of dishevelment: some over here changing clothes, some eating soup or other hot food handed to them by volunteers, some rifling through drop bags to find another layer or pair of socks or some Body Glide or ibuprofen. One guy vomited off to the side, then sat down in a chair by the fire (there was a campfire!). A volunteer asked if they could get him anything and he said, "Just a cup of coffee, please."

A volunteer tried for several minutes to locate my drop bag, and finally I started looking through the assortment of bags laid out on a tarp, eventually finding it, and my pants. What I did, and Jayson did too:

- Spent a minute undoing the safety pins on my race bib, removing it from my shorts

- Took my shoes off

- Put my pants on

- Spent two minutes re-pinning the bib to my pants

All told, we spent a half-hour at the aid station before we left, jogging on a wide dirt road toward the high point of the race.

From the Mile 57.7 aid station, the high point of the race, the course dropped 3,500 feet in 12 miles. We stopped to take off our pants, spending another six or seven minutes removing our shoes and unpinning and re-pinning our race bibs to our shorts, after only wearing the pants for less than six miles.

We jogged down the road in the dark, finding it increasingly difficult to start running again after any period of walking, or stopping to pee. Finishing before the 36-hour cutoff time was definitely not a guarantee at this point.

We passed runners on the road in the dark, and they passed us back a few minutes later. I began to recognize familiar shoes, familiar race vests, familiar body shapes, even one runner's music that droned out of her smartphone speaker whenever we passed her. Is that the same song playing on repeat? Or just the same artist?

Mathematically, we were halfway finished with the race. On paper, we only had one big climb left. The sun would be coming up in a few hours. We'd see our friends at Mile 65, and again at Mile 74. And then we'd have our friends Brody and Forest pacing us for the final 29 miles of the race. These were all very positive data points, and I should have been optimistic. But I was starting to do the math in my head and wow, we still had a long way to go, and not as much time left before the cutoff as I might have hoped. Every time we stopped to walk, talking myself into jogging again, even downhill, felt like dragging myself out of quicksand.

Dr. Kelly Lambert knew that scientific papers had explored the idea that "physical effort used to obtain meaningful rewards is valuable in keeping the brain active and healthy." So she and her students designed an experiment to test the hypothesis, building a four-square-foot room for rats, covering it in bedding used in rat cages.

One group of rats "trained" for five weeks, learning to dig through the bedding to find Froot Loops buried underneath, and thusly connect effort with rewards. A second group of rats was given Froot Loops whether they dug or not. The researchers called the first set of rats "the worker rats" and the second set "the trust fund rats."

After five weeks of training, the researchers put a piece of Froot Loops inside a ventilated cat toy and timed how long rats from each group would "work" on trying to retrieve the Froot Loop reward (which was impossible, but the rats didn't know that). The "worker" rats spent 60 percent more time working on the problem than the "trust fund rats." As Lambert wrote in *The Lab Rat Chronicles*:

"[We] found connections between physical activity and a decreased tendency to give up on life's problems. ... Instead of giving up immediately, the animals that have made strong connections between their behavioral effort and positive consequences appear to be more resilient and resist the temptation to give up."

The Mile 65 aid station looked a bit like a scene from a zombie apocalypse film: dark, in the middle of nowhere, eerily quiet except for a gas-powered generator growling outside one of the race tents, sleeping runners lying on the ground here or there (or maybe dead?), tired friends and family members wandering around probably wishing they were in a warm bed instead of sitting outside in the cold waiting for their idiot friend or relative who was out walking and running through the woods. If there is an opposite of the vibe at an urban road marathon with cheering crowds and bands or DJs blasting music as you run past, the bass vibrating your internal organs, this was it. The mood was grim as we jogged in just before 5 a.m.

Everything was starting to hurt. Every mile after Mile 50 was new terrain for me, but it wasn't so much the miles that were kicking my ass—it was the hours. The longest I'd ever been moving nonstop was about 14 hours, and we were about to begin Hour #22 of who knows how many total hours. I hadn't been up all night since I was in college, save for a couple instances of insomnia when I, in a very different scenario, somehow couldn't sleep in a warm, comfortable bed. Now, we had 38 miles left to cover and I could probably fall asleep standing up in my running shorts if I had a tree to lean on.

Every inch of soft tissue from my toenails up to my hips ached, a low-hum pain that was slowly growing every hour. And I was just plain tired after being awake for almost 24 hours and covering the distance of two and a half marathons, and ups and downs equivalent to 1,400 flights of stairs. We shuffled out of the aid station and jogged downhill for almost five miles as the sun crept toward the horizon. At the next aid station, Mile 69.8, we turned around and started hiking back uphill, headed toward 10,500 feet again, after 23 hours.

The sun came up, the temperature finally stopped dropping, and we started making progress up our last big climb, an unrelenting 3,500 feet up. Were we awash with hope, in the early-morning amber glow of a new day, as the birds around us began their chatter among the trees? No, we were not.

But did we catch sort of a second wind, buoyed by the fact that we had survived 24 hours of constant movement, and could now rely on some new faces, Brody and Forest, to support us for the rest of our race? Again, no.

Jayson was emotional when he sat down at the next aid station, on the verge of tears from all the strain, lack of sleep, and maybe even partly the heartwarming metaphor this race was becoming, for either his life, or our friendship, or both. I was emotionally numb, my mouth hanging open, feeling about 49.9% ready to just quit right there.

If I could sleep for just an hour, I thought as I sat in a camp chair and ate pancakes Hilary had handed to me, voices chattering around me, a blur of encouragement, jokes, laughter, positivity. I did some rough math in my head: A nap, even for a half-hour, would probably jeopardize our chances of finishing before the cutoff. It was either keep moving now and finish with a few minutes or an hour to spare, or try to take a nap now and possibly fuck up the whole thing.

Brody and Forest walked out of the aid station with us, and we hiked up the dirt road in the sun, which already felt too warm.

When a law enforcement officer pulls you over to give you a speeding ticket, they often ask you, "Do you know how fast you were going?" And you always guess low, even if you know exactly how fast you were going. As if it's a negotiation.

I started to notice the exact opposite thing happening: I felt like I was moving quickly—OK, I was barely running at all but wasn't I hiking at a pretty fast clip? No. Time was passing, but we just weren't covering that much ground. It was like we were heading the wrong way on a moving walkway at the airport.

Out on the trails, deep in my own head, I would maybe have liked to believe that I was unique: a person who had developed the endurance to travel long distances on foot without stopping. Of course we all want to believe we're special in some way, and we are, but as a 38-year-old white man who got his kicks running ultramarathon distances, I was the opposite of unique: I was almost exactly the prototypical ultrarunner.

In "The State of Ultra Running 2020[22]," a report by RunRepeat.com and the International Association of Ultrarunners, researchers studied more than 5 million race results from more than 15,000 ultramarathon events worldwide, covering 85 percent of all ultrarunning events in the world from 1996 to 2018.

They found that the average age of ultrarunners worldwide was 42.3 years old, and 77 percent of ultramarathon participants identified as men. (Although in the United States, only 65 percent of ultrarunners were men.) If I looked around at the starting line of any race, I would not be surprised by these stats. Sure, if I got on a flight, chances are I'd be the only person who'd run an ultramarathon, since only .0278 percent of Americans have done so.

Another story I tacitly believed was that I was like Sylvester Stallone's Rocky Balboa: a more-or-less regular guy tromping around out there, teaching myself that through dogged persistence, I was capable of something great, occasionally. Why would I think this? Maybe repeated viewings of the training montages in the first four Rocky movies, in which Rocky punched sides of beef, did one-arm pushups, sweated buckets, grimaced in pain, and hammered himself into the shape of someone who could go the distance with Apollo Creed, Clubber Lang, and Ivan Drago.

Rocky, as it turns out, did run an ultramarathon in *Rocky II*, in the scene famous for his run through the Philadelphia neighborhoods, gradually picking up a huge following of kids, and finally ending at the top of the stairs at the Philadelphia Museum of Art, in a visual so iconic that a statue of Rocky was placed there in 1980. Journalist Dan McQuade, writing for *Philadelphia*[23] magazine in 2013, mapped out the route Rocky supposedly ran in *Rocky II*, having been bothered for years at how convoluted it was. The total distance Rocky covered in his run, in a gray sweatsuit, headband, and Chuck Taylors, was 30.6 miles.

A 21st century Rocky Balboa for endurance runners might look more like Jaybie Pagarigan, a 4-foot 11-inch, 39-year-old Filipino woman profiled in the *New York Times*[24] in 2019. Pagarigan, who worked six days a week as a domestic worker for a Hong Kong family, was one of many "helpers" who had not only taken up trail running, but was starting to succeed in trail and ultramarathon races around Hong Kong.

The more than 380,000 foreign domestic helpers working in Hong Kong make up 5 percent of the country's population, despite being prohibited from applying for permanent residency. They're required to live with their employers, and although they often have their own bedrooms, their bedrooms often double as storage closets, laundry rooms, or offices.

With running, immigrant helpers like Pagarigan explored a different identity. "Trail running has emerged as something of an unlikely equalizer for domestic workers," Mary Hui wrote in the Times story. "For at least a few hours, the sweat and camaraderie of the trails blur the lines between employers and maids, and among locals, migrants and expatriates."

Pagarigan, occupied six days a week with her work as a live-in helper, still found time to train, getting up at 4:30 a.m. to head out the door and run up Mount Butler, the 1,430-foot forested peak rising above Hong Kong's Eastern District, finishing the 5-mile round trip before 6 a.m. She mixed in running with some of her work errands, running to and from the market to buy fresh produce, then running up 18 flights of stairs to the apartment with full shopping bags. On Sundays, her one day off, she'd hike or run the nearby trails, or compete in races.

Jayson's ankle had started hurting around Mile 70, and it was getting worse. He was starting to limp a little bit, then the limp became more pronounced, then he just stopped talking altogether.

I kept shuffling along as the sun climbed. I was sweating again, the water in my bottles warmed by the sun. I chatted intermittently with Forest, Brody, and Jayson, trying to stay positive, but I was in my own head the entire time, repeating a thought pattern in 20-second intervals.

I remembered that on this same section of the course, when we had passed through during the night, I had seen a vault toilet on the right side of the road somewhere around the 82-mile aid station, Summit Lake. I was starting to have a pretty grumpy stomach and was looking forward to a toilet, any kind of toilet. Just before the final turn in the road before Summit Lake, it appeared, hallelujah, and I walked up to it, to find the door unlocked and the toilet unoccupied. I stood inside the door for a second, adjusting to the dim light, holding my breath a little, and bracing for the total lack of air movement inside the tiny building.

No toilet paper, just three empty cardboard rolls. No toilet paper on the floor, no half roll of toilet paper left by a good Samaritan camper, not a shred of an old newspaper, nothing. Now, I can poop in the wild, using sticks and rocks for toilet paper, no problem. But you can't bring rocks into a vault toilet and use them as toilet paper (they don't biodegrade and can't be pumped out of the toilet during its cleaning later). I sighed, opened the door, and walked out into the midday sun.

A group of people on horseback ambled by on the road and asked how I was doing. I said Wonderful, How Are You, and they asked how many miles I had left. I said 21 miles, and someone said, "You got it. Anyone can run 21 miles." I said thanks.

I walked into the EZ-up shelter at the Summit Lake aid station and tried to squeeze into a corner of shade. Brody filled my water bottles and demanded I eat a plate of pancakes. Another runner sat in a chair and complained about how bad he felt.

"At this point," he said, "I'm just trying to think of a way to get disqualified so I don't have to finish." Jayson looked up from his chair and just said, "Huh." I thought: We have to get away from this guy.

I got up from my chair and walked to the end of the parking lot behind some trees, dug up a loose rock and squatted over the hole to poop. It was my only option. I walked back to the aid station and pumped some hand sanitizer onto my hands. Jayson and I started back up the trail, a short but steep climb into the sun at 10,400 feet before it leveled off and rolled into scattered tree cover.

In 2017, *Trail Runner Magazine's* Doug Mayer interviewed Jay Sanguinetti[25], a research assistant professor at the University of New Mexico, about hallucinations that ultrarunners sometimes experience during long races. Sanguinetti said that when we see things that aren't there, it's just the brain misinterpreting information from the optic nerve. Data comes in through the eyes, and the brain pieces together what it is, based on experience. Experience, and sometimes expectations, or "top-down" factors, which can affect what we "see":

"It's like going into a house that you think is haunted," Sanguinetti said. "You expect to see ghosts, so you see ghosts. Then, you freak out and expend a lot of energy on being aroused."

Around Mile 95, as the trail wound around corners near the top of Mt. Werner, I began to see tents popping out of the trees, my brain desperately wanting the last aid station to appear, signaling that we were at the top and had just six all-downhill miles remaining. I spotted a corner of a tent sticking out of the foliage a half-dozen times over several minutes, and when I blinked or looked away for a second, they'd disappear.

It was not all downhill from the final aid station at Mile 96.9. Jayson's ankle hurt so much he couldn't jog down the steep service roads zigzagging their way down the west-facing slopes of the ski resort. Even walking hurt. Finally, he figured out that walking backward was the least painful option.

I could have left him, since I wasn't injured, and could jog just fine. You could argue that a true friend would never leave him to struggle to the finish on his own.

I was, however, nowhere near thinking about what a true friend would do. I just didn't fucking care anymore. Staying with him meant I could walk instead of run. Running hurt, and walking hurt a little less. It took longer, but it hurt a little less.

Between the four of us, we started to talk about the math: Did we have enough time to make it to the finish before the 36-hour mark, walking backward? Maybe, maybe not. Might be best to at least run some of it, just to hedge our bets.

Jayson turned around and started running. I watched him for a few seconds, then reluctantly shuffled into a slow jog. Bolts of pain shot up my legs, quadrupling the pain I felt while walking. I kept going as long as Jayson kept jogging, and walked when he walked.

With a little over a mile to go, the roads started to flatten out, and Brody and Forest ran ahead to the finish line, leaving us to do the rest on our own. We jogged, Jayson hucking himself forward on his trekking poles, trying in vain to keep the weight off his ankle.

We ran with halted strides through the finish arch, Jayson grimacing in pain, and as we passed under it, we finally stopped. Thirty-five hours, 27 minutes, and 20 seconds. We'd made it with 32 minutes to spare, and a few minutes of daylight remaining. Jayson burst into tears, and Fred, the race director, standing ready to hug every runner who came through the arch, choked back tears.

I didn't feel anything, aside from relief. I didn't care if we were dead last. We ended up tied for 132nd place out of 145 finishers. I just wanted to sit down.

Fred grabbed two small boxes containing finisher belt buckles and handed them to us, and we plopped down in camp chairs two feet past the finish line, a couple of utterly destroyed rats, each with his Froot Loop in hand.

After a few minutes, we moved away from the finish line, shuffling over to another set of camp chairs our friends had brought, and a couple deep dish pizzas Debi had ordered. The light faded from the sky, and we slowly walked to the parking garage in the dark to go back to the condo and sleep like two people who didn't have to worry about a 100-mile race anymore.

III.

I tied my shoes, walked down the stairs from our condo, and started jogging for the first time in 26 days since the Run Rabbit Run. I shuffled around the crushed-rock path under the big old trees in Cheesman Park, wondering how many laps I'd done there. I cruised around the neighborhood, in no rush to do anything besides run a ways and see how it felt. The anxiety of preparing for a 100-mile race was gone. My legs were fine. I ran 3.5 miles, for the first time in a long time without feeling like it was my job.

For a week after the race, I had walked to the grocery store or to a coffee shop, but never put on my running shoes. Three days post-race, Brody texted to check in. I said I didn't feel too bad, just waiting to see if I felt any injuries when the endorphins wore off, but surprisingly, nothing hurt that badly yet. He texted back: "Maybe this is in your blood and it's what you're supposed to be doing."

That was an encouraging thing for him to write, but: really? Didn't we just barely finish? I didn't feel like we had accomplished something—I felt like we had survived it. And just by the skin of our teeth, with a half-hour to spare. Or: Was that how it felt for most people?

Jayson's ankle was still hurting, which was not surprising since it had started flaring up with 30-plus miles to go and he'd finished anyway. I could barely wrap my head around finishing those last miles without any injuries, so I was in awe of his grit. When I stopped over at his apartment to check on him, he was hobbling around, using trekking poles for support. Twenty days after he limped across the finish line, he went out and hiked and ran four miles on trails at Matthews-Winters Park near Denver.

In the years after we crossed the Run Rabbit Run finish line, Jayson attempted two other 100-mile races, withdrawing around the 80-mile mark due to the same ankle pain—but in a different ankle each time. He was eventually diagnosed with hypermobile Ehlers-Danlos Syndrome, a genetic connective-tissue disorder whose symptoms can include overly flexible joints. It helped him do yoga, but was not ideal for ultramarathon running.

I felt OK, but you couldn't pay me enough money to even think about signing up for another 100-mile race. I had to admit, though, surviving it with no major injuries was encouraging. Even Jayson's ankle healed up fairly quickly, all things considered. I mean, neither of us had to be hauled away from the finish line of a 100-mile race in a wheelchair, and that wasn't nothing, right?

In 2011, Gary "Lazarus Lake" Cantrell started a new type of race on his property in Bell Buckle, Tennessee. He named it Big Dog's Backyard Ultra, after his adopted pit bull, Big. The rules were straightforward: Runners had one hour to complete a 4.16667-mile trail loop. They could run as fast as they wanted, or as slowly as they wanted, as long as they finished under the one-hour mark. Because at the one-hour mark, Cantrell blew his whistle, and runners had to line up and run the loop again, in one hour or less. They repeated the process every hour until there was only one person left. This race was the invention of the "backyard ultra," or "last person standing" race—in which contestants kept going until everyone quit, except the last person remaining, who was the winner. Cantrell's course is 4.16667 miles because in 24 hours of running one loop per hour, runners will cover 100 miles. The loop is on rolling terrain, with tight turns and plenty of rocks and roots to step over and around.

In its inaugural year, Tim Englund won the race, completing 18 laps, or 75 miles. He won again in 2013, almost doubling his first win total, with 35 laps (145.8 miles). In 2018, Johan Steene of Sweden won, covering just over 283 miles in 68 laps. The first woman to win, Maggie Guterl, completed 60 laps (250 miles), and in 2021, Harvey Lewis won, breaking the record with 354 miles in 85 laps, or three and a half straight days of running one lap per hour. In 2023, Lewis completed 107 laps along with Ukranian Ihor Verys, who had been completing each lap faster than Lewis. Both runners started lap 108, after four days and 11 hours of running, and shortly after, Verys returned to the start/finish area, bowing out of the race. Lewis finished his 108th loop, breaking his own record with 450 miles run in 108 hours, or four and a half days.

The novel *Carrie* launched Stephen King's career in 1974, selling more than four million copies in paperback, and becoming the first of King's works to be adapted into a film, grossing more than $33 million at the box office.

But *Carrie* wasn't King's first novel. He had written several, none of which had been published yet. One of them he'd started writing in 1966 as a freshman at the University of Maine, and rewritten several times, but hadn't sold yet. It was finally published in 1979 under a pseudonym, Richard Bachman. The title was *The Long Walk*, and above the title on the first edition cover, the text read: "In a future America, the marathon is the ultimate sports competition—a novel of chilling, macabre possibility."

In the dystopian future of *The Long Walk*, an annual walking contest is the most-watched even in America: One hundred teenage boys are selected to walk along U.S. Route 1, starting at the U.S.-Canada border. If a Walker's speed drops below four miles per hour for more than 30 seconds, a team of soldiers pacing the boys in a vehicle warns the Walker. If a Walker receives three warnings and doesn't speed up 30 seconds after the final warning, the soldiers shoot and kill him.

At the beginning of the event, The Major, the head of the secret police force and the creator of The Long Walk, addresses the boys, saying, "I give my congratulations to the winner among your number, and my acknowledgements of valor to the losers."

The Long Walk continues until there is only one survivor, who wins a cash prize and whatever he wants for the rest of his life.

King doesn't cite an actual mileage total for the winner of The Long Walk in the book, but Pat Coston, a web developer from New Jersey, spent a year and a half documenting the route, hiring someone to gather the data and building a detailed website page of notes. He also drove the entire route over two days, and calculated the winner walked 461 miles over the course of 115.25 straight hours[26].

I had just drunk the last sips of water from the bottle on my bike when we hit the asphalt ribbon of Grand View Point Road, cutting across the red desert atop Island in the Sky mesa in Canyonlands National Park near Moab. Hilary and I had decided to ride the 100-mile dirt loop of White Rim Road over four days, without a vehicle, which meant we'd carried 15 liters of water each on our bikes and backpacks on the first day, and then conserved it the whole time to make it last. It was unseasonably warm that Thanksgiving, even for the southern Utah desert, sunny with highs in the 50s, but we had made it work. With six miles of pedaling to go to our car, the end was in sight. So was a runner, coming at us, shuffling along on our side of the road.

It was the same guy we had seen the day before, down on White Rim Road. I remembered the burgundy Ultimate Direction backpack.

The White Rim is a popular dirt-road tour that drops down from the Island in the Sky mesa onto the White Rim Sandstone formation and winds in and out, tracing a cliff edge for more than 70 miles. All along the White Rim, you can see the water of the Colorado River and later the Green River, but you can't access it because of the impassable cliffs at the edge of the White Rim. Most people who ride the White Rim take mountain bikes and have a friend drive a truck or a jeep carrying their water, food, and camping gear, and ride 20 or 30 miles a day, and do the entire length of the road over three days. Some mountain bikers will ride the entire White Rim, plus about 30 miles of additional dirt and asphalt road to make a full 100-mile loop, in a single long day. I had thought our plan—carrying all our water, on bikes with no suspension—was a little out there. But this guy: Was he running the whole thing?

I was sure the runner coming toward us, again, was doing the same loop, in the opposite direction as we were. As he approached, I could see the quick shuffling steps of someone battling deep fatigue. I asked, "Are you doing the White Rim?" and he replied yes, he had cached some water down there about 60 miles into his route, and was now down to the final five miles to his car. He said it had gone pretty well, but his backpack, when it was full of water, weighed 20 pounds, so that hadn't been ideal. But overall he was doing great. I asked if he needed anything, not sure what I could give him since I'd just run out of water myself, and he said no thanks, he was good.

Not wanting to hold him up, I wished him luck, and pedaled on. He had just run his own, completely unsupported, 100-mile ultramarathon, out in the desert, just to do it.

Forest messaged me about a race in North Carolina at the beginning of March: The Fontandango 50-miler. The course was a 10-mile loop in the Yellow Creek Mountains, with about 2,000 feet of elevation gain per loop. We'd run five loops, for 50 miles and 10,000 feet of elevation gain—almost exactly half of the Run Rabbit Run.

We would be in the area anyway, doing some photo shoots for a book project Forest and I were working on. It would be sort of a whirlwind trip, going from Asheville to Cumberland Island in Georgia, then Savannah, then Little Tybee Island off the coast of Georgia, and then up to the Red River Gorge in Kentucky. The day before the race, we'd drive five hours to a hotel in North Carolina, eat some sandwiches in our hotel rooms, and wake up at 5:30 a.m. the next morning for the start of the 50-mile race at 7 a.m.

We signed up in January, about seven weeks before the race, and I tried to train the best I could, in between other travel. I managed a couple 20-plus mile runs, and then one 31-mile run with 5,000 feet of elevation gain, two weeks before the race, going up and down Green Mountain near Denver five times on a fortuitously dry Valentine's Day, only stopping to refill my water at the car once.

The plan was: Hilary would run the 50K race, which started at 8 a.m. Forest and I would run the 50-mile race, along with Forest's younger, very fast brother, Canyon, who had placed second in the Fontandango 50K the year before, and had won and finished in the top three of several regional mountain trail races. After the race, Hilary and I would drive two hours to a hotel near the Asheville airport, where we had a flight home at 5:58 a.m. the next morning.

I tried to say that it was a bad plan, that I was not a fast runner, and that I would hold up Forest and Canyon. This was true. What I did not think of: In addition to holding them up, they would pull me along to go faster than I normally would. Or, rather, push me to go faster. Drag me? Yes, drag.

I had first met Forest on a charity climb of Mt. Whitney in 2012. He had grown up homeschooled in the mountains of western North Carolina, and was just starting his career as an adventure photographer. He was six years younger than me, and from not too far away, looked like Orlando Bloom in *Pirates of the Caribbean*: flowing brown curly hair, brown eyes, square jaw, athlete's build. He was living in Brooklyn then, and when I visited New York later that summer, I reached out and we got together to boulder in Central Park, surf at Rockaway Beach, and take the bus up to New Paltz to climb the quartz conglomerate cliffs at the Shawangunks. Our proudest work was a "food marathon," in which we traversed Manhattan and Brooklyn, starting at Absolute Bagels at 108th and Broadway and running 20ish miles, stopping to eat eight iconic New York foods along the way: Bagel, egg cream, knish, hot dog, street pretzel, doughnut, cheesecake, and pizza.

Forest was a great photographer, or more accurately, a wrangler of light. He didn't use lens filters, or even lens caps, and his approach to working seemed seat-of-the-pants, including booking everything last-minute, doing office work in the passenger seats of rental cars as we drove around the West, stuffing backpacks with way too much of everything, and bringing the most inexcusable shit into the backcountry for a photo shoot: a pair of heavy slippers, a quart of half-and-half, a jar of tapenade. He would create photos, and I would write, and we'd put together a story. Later, we made short films together. Our approaches to almost everything were completely opposite. I had never run a car out of gas in my entire life, and he had done it dozens of times. Once, traveling across Utah in my car, which Forest was driving, we talked about this, as I hadn't been looking at the gas gauge and we were perilously close to a completely dry gas tank. Forest told me a story:

"One of those times I ran out of gas," Forest said, "I got out of the car and there was a gas can sitting off to the side of the road, and I had pulled over just down the hill from a gas station. So I grabbed the gas can, jogged up to the gas station, filled it up, and the whole thing only cost me about 15 minutes." Fittingly, he had been on his way to the airport in that story, and he still made his flight, but just barely.

I had seen Forest pilot a raft through the Grand Canyon's terrifying rapids, run up and down mountains, climb difficult rock and ice, and almost always capture beautiful photos while doing it. I don't know how we managed to get along so well, but I'd like to think we rubbed off a little bit on each other, and maybe I learned to take things a little easier, and he became a little more punctual. And perhaps I got a little faster. Not enough to keep up with him, but still, maybe a little faster.

They said it would be fun, a 50-mile race in some of the mountains they had grown up exploring, a small local event with a few dozen runners who liked steep stuff.

It was fun, for several hours. On the final lap, I was not feeling great, and wanted to get off the Forest + Canyon train, but they refused to leave me. Just as dusk hit, I grabbed a small cup of soda from the course's only aid station and walked away, slurping the first Mountain Dew I'd had in at least 15 years, who knows why, I guess it just sounded good. Within a couple minutes, I was off to the side of the trail, hoping no other runners would come along in the 120 seconds or so it took me to empty my bowels and bury the evidence.

It was a bad plan. We continued on, despite my continued suggestions that I should just finish by myself, don't worry about little old me, I'll be fine, go on without me, I'll see you at the finish line. But no, they insisted.

We crossed the finish line together at 8:02 p.m., headlamps shining in the dark, tied for 20th place out of 26 runners, Canyon's worst trail race result ever, by far. But he didn't care. It was the worst I'd felt in a long time, maybe ever. Everybody does something, usually anyway. We thought we would do this and it would be fun.

By the time we took photos, packed up, and said a hurried goodbye, it was almost 9 p.m. Our 6 a.m. flight was in nine hours, but of course we'd need to be there by 4:30, 5:00 at the latest. I had just burned about 10,000 calories during the race, so we needed to get some food, too. My stomach was a bit dodgy, but I didn't really have a choice. Plus I love Waffle House.

I was trashed, feeling very drowsy driving the rental van on the curvy mountain roads in the dark, but we made it halfway to Asheville before we stopped at the Waffle House in Sylva for $20 worth of eggs, hash browns, and waffles. I drank some coffee, thinking it would help me stay awake for the drive, but there was no way it would keep me up once I plopped my head on a hotel pillow.

After the Waffle House, we made it down the road another few minutes before it became clear we needed to stop for the night. We checked into a hotel, dragged our bags inside, and were finally able to stop moving and relax for a few hours. I was ready to sleep. My digestive system was ready for a different kind of party.

The Executioner's Song by Norman Mailer is a 1,076-page book and what many consider to be Mailer's magnum opus, and a master work of reporting, detailing the troubled life, crimes, and murder trial of Gary Gilmore, who was the first person to be executed after the federal reinstatement of the death penalty in 1976. Gilmore not only wanted to plead guilty, he wanted to be executed, and he wanted to be executed by firing squad.

Larry Schiller, a photographer and journalist, had acquired the exclusive book and film rights to Gary Gilmore's story. Schiller would be there when Gilmore was executed in January 1977, and as the date approached, seemingly every media outlet in the country wanted to buy Schiller's firsthand account of the events that day. As Mailer wrote, the decision to sell or not sell the account, for up to $125,000 (about $525,000 in 2021), tore Schiller up inside, literally:

Schiller walked to the window again. The snow was coming down hard by now and he was tired. His hand ached from squeezing the phone. He started crying. He could not explain what it was about, or why he was crying, but it went through him uncontrollably.

He said to himself, "I don't know any longer whether what I'm doing is morally right," and that made him cry even more. He had been saying to himself for weeks that he was not part of the circus, that he had instincts which raised him above, a desire to record history, true history, not journalistic crap, but now he felt as if he was finally part of the circus and might even be the biggest part of it, and in the middle of crying, he went into the bathroom and took the longest fucking shit of his life. It was all diarrhea. His system, after days of running nonstop and nights with crummy sleep, was by now totally screwed up. The horrors were loose. The diarrhea went through him as if to squeeze every last rotten thing out, and still it came. When he thought he might be done, he looked out the window at the snow and made the decision that in no way was he ever going to sell Gary Gilmore's execution. No. No way could anybody convince him. He would not make that fucking mistake for greed or security. No. He didn't care if he never saw a penny at the end. He had to stay by what his gut told him.

After one of my many trips to the bathroom in our hotel room that night, I checked my phone to see a text message from United Airlines that had arrived at 11:54 p.m.:

Your flight to Chicago (UA5162) is canceled due to aircraft maintenance. We've rebooked you on an alternate itinerary.

< 26266 >

Mar 3, 2018, 9:54 PM

1of3 Your flight to Chicago (UA5162) is canceled due to aircraft maintenance. We've rebooked you on an alternate itinerary.

2of3 We've rebooked you for Mar. 5 on our 558am flight via Chicago (UA5162), arriving in Denver at 931am.

3of3 See full details, view other options and check in at https://myua.co/2oNG7Pb

I went back to sleep, for once being thankful for a 24-hour flight delay.

If you stand at the South Rim of the Grand Canyon, near the Grand Canyon Village ice cream shop whose windows sit about 40 feet from the rock wall at the edge of the drop-off into the canyon, you can see the other side, the North Rim. It's only about 11 miles away from where you're standing, as the crow flies—or maybe more aptly, as the California Condor flies. By foot, though, it's about 25 miles from where you're standing holding your ice cream cone, and by car, it's four hours away. If you don't have wings, crossing the canyon is a time-consuming undertaking.

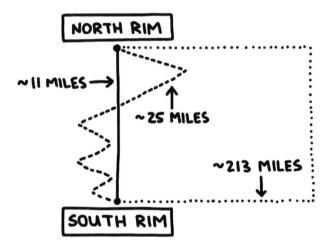

I didn't sign up for another race for a year after the Fontandango 50. I didn't feel like I wanted to squeeze in one more big commitment, along with the training, and the anxiety. There was an opening on my calendar in April, though, a little over a month after the Fontandango 50, when I would be in northern Arizona for work, with a few days off. I messaged my friend Mitsu and asked if he'd like to try running the Rim-to-Rim-to-Rim in the Grand Canyon.

Doing the Rim-to-Rim-to-Rim is kind of like doing your own ultramarathon, except there are no crews, no aid stations, no course markers, and no official, well, anything. The gist is this: You start on one side of the Grand Canyon, run down to the bottom, cross the Colorado River, run/hike up the other side of the Grand Canyon, turn around, run back down to the bottom, cross the Colorado River again, and run/hike back up to your car. Depending on which trails you use, it's roughly between 42 and 47 miles, with around 11,700 feet of elevation gain. If you go the long way, the elevation profile looks like this:

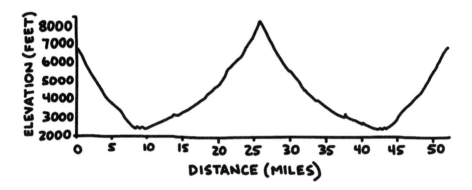

As far as places to do a self-supported ultramarathon, the Grand Canyon is arguably pretty friendly: there's literally running water coming out of spigots at several points on a couple of the more-trafficked trails (and if you time it right, all of them will be turned on), the trails are well-marked so it's hard to get lost, it's in a national park, it's in the desert so it's usually dry and rain and snow are generally pretty predictable, and there are enough passing hikers that you can usually get help if something minor comes up. If you time it right, you can swing into the canteen at Phantom Ranch, at the bottom of the canyon, for a coffee, lemonade, or beer in the middle of your run.

It is, however, a really shitty place to sprain your ankle, or have a heart attack, or run out of water. If you need to be evacuated for any reason, it's not like an ambulance is a few minutes away, because there are no roads through the canyon. Mail is delivered to Phantom Ranch by mule. Raft trips through the canyon carry satellite phones or ground-to-air radios, and if they have a medical emergency, they literally call a passing commercial airline flying over the canyon, and then the airline pilots call the National Park Service to facilitate a helicopter rescue. Every year, between 250 and 300 visitors have to be rescued by the NPS. Conversely, thousands of park visitors don't have to be rescued each year.

Mitsu and I hopped out of the car at the South Rim at 4:35 a.m., pushing hard to get the car doors open in the constant wind. In the dark, under a dome of stars, I pulled on a beanie and gloves, swung on my running vest, bulging with water bottles and 4,000-plus calories' worth of snacks, and started hiking toward the trailhead in running shorts and a wind jacket, hoping the wind would calm when we started down the trail into the canyon.

We had decided to go the long way, 47 miles instead of 42 miles, because the logistics were easier going down the Bright Angel Trail, the most popular hiking trail in the park, than the other way—the South Kaibab Trail.

Mitsu took off down the trail at a fast pace, bounding through the darkness, light from his headlamp flashing off the canyon wall. The trail has steep drop-offs in spots, but it's generally really wide, so you'd really have to lose control to fall, or be drunk. About three miles down this trail, I once talked to a guy who was backpacking down to Phantom Ranch on a hot September Saturday, and he pulled a can of Busch Light out of his pack and started drinking it, proud to only be hydrating with beer. He offered me one, and I declined, but I kind of wondered how many he had in his backpack.

When you view the Grand Canyon from the South Rim, as almost all visitors do, you stand high on one side of it and look down into it. You can sort of wrap your head around how vast and complex it is as your gaze moves from the internal buttes and mesas that rise up out of it, and the dozens of side canyons that pour into the main channel of the Colorado River. But you don't see the Colorado River from any point on the South Rim unless you drive to Desert View, because of how vast, deep, and convoluted the canyon and its side canyons are.

The Rim-to-Rim-to-Rim condenses the experience of Grand Canyon into one long day: Runners use three of the most well-maintained trails in the canyon, in two drainage paths that are approximately a straight shot, and the only two bridges that span the Colorado River, and use them to cross the canyon, almost perpendicular to the river's route through the canyon. If you tried to randomly pick two other side canyons and make your way across, you'd have to bushwhack, almost certainly use technical canyoneering gear (and skills), and swim across the river at the bottom, and it would probably take days, if you didn't just fail and/or die. There is one other direct path from the South to North Rim several miles to the west, using the much less-maintained Bass Trails, but there's no bridge across, so if you do it, you have to swim across the chilly river, which is 50 degrees year-round because it comes out of the bottom of the Glen Canyon Dam. So when you get your ass kicked doing the Rim-to-Rim-to-Rim, it's kind of funny to think that it's the easiest way across.

We tried to run, but the big stair-steps built into the trail every few feet made it difficult to have any sort of consistent rhythm, so we ended up intermittently running and hiking down. Mitsu almost immediately had pain in one of his hamstrings, and started to wonder if he strained something. We saw no one for the first three miles, until two backpackers leaving the Havasupai Garden campground on their hike out appeared as the first hints of sunlight started to illuminate the canyon.

The Bright Angel Trail leaves the South Rim and descends through millions of years of geologic history in a few short miles: At the top, the trail cuts through white cliffs of 270-million-year-old Kaibab Limestone, and nine miles of winding later, crosses the river at the Bright Angel Bridge, looking at 1.7 billion-year-old Vishnu Schist.

We hit the bottom of the canyon around 7:00, crossing the silver bridge across the Colorado River, and taking the trail through the Bright Angel Campground, and then past the cabins and canteen at Phantom Ranch. A few miles past Phantom Ranch, Mitsu decided it would be better to not push his hamstring. He would head back to Phantom Ranch and wait for me at the canteen and re-join me when I came through again in five or six or seven hours.

I kept jogging as the sun rose, making my way up to the North Rim. A 47-mile day with this much climbing and descending, while carrying everything I needed with me, was a big reach for me, but I had traveled the Rim-to-Rim, one-way, North Rim to South Rim, twice before, once on a three-day backpacking trip, and once hiking and running with my friend Greg. So in theory, I sort of knew what I was getting into.

It seemed like a natural step in progression as well: I had figured out how to cover 31 miles with the help of aid stations, volunteers, and course markings. Then 50 miles, and then 100 miles. A run of almost 50 miles on familiar terrain, with access to running water in a few spots, seemed doable. I had tons of calories in my vest, a space blanket to wrap myself in should I have some sort of accident or need to spend the night outside, and iodine tablets in case I needed to purify water from a creek.

Just before 11:30 a.m., after a little over four hours of nonstop hiking and running, I popped out of the canyon on the North Rim at the trailhead parking lot, where I found a trash can and a water spigot, which, fortuitously, had been turned on. My legs were tired, but the next 14 miles were all downhill, I told myself. I emptied the pockets of my vest, tossing my wrappers into the trash can, filled my bottles, and started to jog down the trail.

The switchbacking North Kaibab Trail grabbed my attention on the way down, the canyon opening in front of me as I coasted down the singletrack I'd hiked up minutes earlier. At a few spots where the trail had been cut into red sandstone cliffsides, I slowed down and watched my feet—tripping and pitching off the trail to the left could mean a fall of a few dozen to a few hundred feet. Thanks to the high winds that morning, the trails were not crowded. I hadn't seen another hiker in seven miles, so even if I landed in the most forgiving spot below and could yell for help, it was pretty unlikely anyone would hear me. Note to self: Falling off a cliff would be a huge bummer.

My legs started to feel more and more pins and needles of fatigue as the canyon walls narrowed along my path. I began looking forward to crossing the river again so I could slow down and hike uphill and use different muscles. The sun was high, and the breeze helped, but I was still heating up. I was not feeling great. As I jogged along through the steep, tight walls of The Box, the narrow inner gorge of Vishnu Schist that winds along Bright Angel Creek for the final five miles to Phantom Ranch, I started to fantasize about all the possible ways I could get out of doing the final 10 to 12 miles of the Rim-To-Rim-To-Rim:

- Hike back up to the North Rim and convince someone to give me a ride (4 hours) back to the South Rim (more distance + elevation gain than going to South Rim)

- Stop at Phantom Ranch and try to get a room in one of the cabins (unlikely)

- Go just past Phantom Ranch to the Bright Angel Campground and see if anyone camping there has an "extra sleeping bag" (even more unlikely)

- Go into the Bright Angel Campground bathroom, lock the stall, sit down on the toilet, and sleep (possible)

- Convince a National Park Service employee that I require a helicopter rescue from the bottom of the canyon

Was I tired? Incredibly. Did I feel like I couldn't go on? I mean, kind of.

In October 2009, a group of four hikers—two men and their teenage sons—went into the canyon on an arduous backpacking trip, and carried a SPOT satellite tracking device that they'd rented in case of emergency. At some point, they pressed the "HELP" button on the device, which is an SOS signal. The National Park Service began to initiate a rescue the following day, and a helicopter flew into their remote location. Upon arrival, the group told the would-be rescuers that they'd pressed the HELP button because they ran out of water, but it was OK, because they'd found a water source now. Later that evening, they pressed the button again, this time about a quarter-mile from where rescuers had contacted them that morning. An Arizona Department of Public Safety helicopter flew in and used night-vision goggles in order to locate the group, who, this time, said they were worried about getting dehydrated because their water "tasted salty." They asked to be rescued, and the helicopter crew declined, but left them with some water. The next morning, the group pressed the HELP button again, and the park service finally evacuated them via helicopter. Once evacuated, the group refused medical assessment or treatment[27].

Even as I got closer to Phantom Ranch, four miles to go, then three, I started to have trouble motivating myself to keep running. I let myself walk a minute here, another minute there, in between running. I'd pull out my phone to take a photo, telling myself it was OK to walk because the photo would come out better, and then I'd take my sweet time putting my phone back in my vest pocket, and suddenly I'd been walking for almost a minute, just to take one photo. My feet were not bloody stumps at the end of my legs. I was not slowly dying of a gunshot wound. I didn't even have debilitating blisters. I was just tired of moving.

Joseph Campbell, a literature professor at Sarah Lawrence College from 1934 to 1972, studied comparative mythology and comparative religion, and hero myth patterns. He became famous for his theory of the monomyth, or "the hero's journey," a template for hero stories common in epic poems, books, movies, and religions of the world. In Campbell's words, the gist is:

"A hero ventures forth from the world of common day into a region of supernatural wonder: fabulous forces are there encountered and a decisive victory is won: the hero comes back from this mysterious adventure with the power to bestow boons on his fellow man."

Examples: Luke Skywalker in *Star Wars*, Dorothy in *The Wizard of Oz*, Jane in *Jane Eyre*, anyone who climbs Mt. Everest and becomes a motivational speaker.

A basic diagram of Campbell's theory of The Hero's Journey:

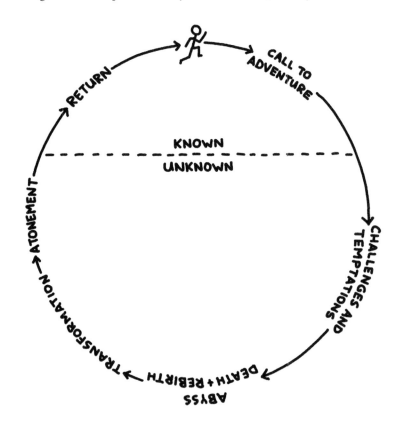

If doing the Rim-to-Rim-to-Rim was a story, and that story was the hero's journey, then in that story, I would be the hero on the journey across the canyon. Hero, though, is a bit lofty, for someone voluntarily doing something strenuous. Was Don Quixote a hero? Maybe if I was The One Person Who Could Defeat The Villain Intent On Using A Superweapon To Destroy Civilization. But I wasn't. I was just a guy running across a canyon with a vest full of snacks.

Kurt Vonnegut had some different ideas about how stories were structured, and often illustrated them during lectures using charts he drew on chalkboards, and in his final book, *Man Without a Country*. One of those story structures he called "Man in Hole," and it is very simple: A person gets into trouble, then gets out of it. It looks like this:

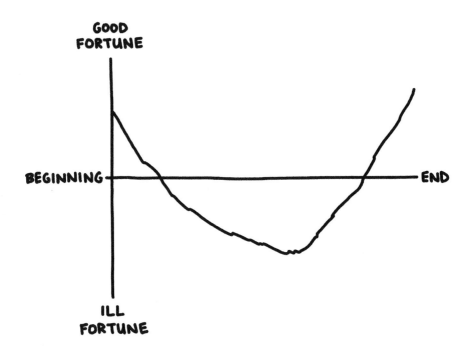

The Rim-to-Rim-to-Rim was a trap, and I was stuck in it. To get out of the trap, I had to gnaw my own leg off—just metaphorically, of course. Also, I had set the trap myself:

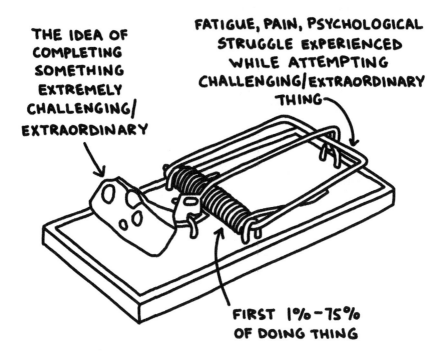

THE IDEA OF COMPLETING SOMETHING EXTREMELY CHALLENGING/ EXTRAORDINARY

FATIGUE, PAIN, PSYCHOLOGICAL STRUGGLE EXPERIENCED WHILE ATTEMPTING CHALLENGING/EXTRAORDINARY THING

FIRST 1% - 75% OF DOING THING

When I walked in the door of the canteen at Phantom Ranch, Mitsu sat up from his seat at a table near the window, looking a bit restless. He was still nursing the remnants of an Arnold Palmer and asked if I'd like anything to drink. I had previously talked about sitting down to double-fist a coffee and a lemonade at the canteen, thinking it would be both relaxing and refreshing before the last uphill leg of the day, but now, it seemed like sitting down for any length of time might be dangerous, in that I might not want to stand up before dark. So we walked out the door and started heading toward the river.

We crossed the bridge again, hiking along the sandy trail on a shelf about 50 feet above the river, and then a snake fell out of the sky and bounced off Mitsu's shoulder before landing on the trail and slithering away. Mitsu jumped in surprise, I jumped at his jumping in surprise, and then we both started laughing when we realized it wasn't a rattlesnake. I wondered if the snake was embarrassed for accidentally falling off the ledge above us.

The trail we had flown down just after dawn that morning had turned into a never-ending staircase. By my count, it was my seventh time going up the Bright Angel trail, and I knew the parts that always felt longer than the others, and that when you get to Havasupai Garden, you've done half the mileage back up to the South Rim, but only one-third of the elevation gain, and the steepest part is ahead. Running was out of the question. We just kept hiking, but quickly, to hopefully make it out of the canyon before dark.

Eventually, the white cliffs of Kaibab Limestone, the final geologic layer before the trail turned into a sidewalk on the South Rim, appeared just above us, and we trudged up the final switchbacks, popping out of the canyon five minutes after sunset, with enough dusky daylight to walk to the car without using headlamps.

Somebody told me a joke once that went something like this:

Them: You know what the best vodka is?

Me: What?

Them: It's a joke. There is no good vodka.

This joke is funny if you don't like vodka, but it's also about the concept of acquired tastes. Vodka, like almost all liquor, is not something most five-year-olds would say tastes "good," compared to, say, chocolate milk. But adults know vodka will make them feel good, because it contains alcohol. So we learn to like it—even if we still only like it enough to drink it when it's mixed at a 1:3 ratio with grapefruit juice.

In 2019, 74.1 million 9-liter cases of vodka were sold in the United States, which amounted to $6.6 billion in sales for vodka distillers[28].

Jeffrey Steingarten became *Vogue* magazine's food critic in 1989, which was great for him, except that he hated kimchi, the national pickle of Korea. And also any food that featured dill. And swordfish, anchovies, lard, falafel, clams, refried beans, any blue food (besides berries and plums), and a few other things. In the introduction of his book, *The Man Who Ate Everything*, he wrote[29]:

By design and by destiny, humans are omnivores. Our teeth and digestive systems are all-purpose and ready for anything. Our genes do not dictate what foods we should find tasty or repulsive. We come into the world with a yen for sweet (newborns can even distinguish among glucose, fructose, lactose, and sucrose) and a weak aversion to bitterness, and after four months develop a fondness for salt. Some people are born particularly sensitive to one taste or odor; others have trouble digesting milk sugar or wheat gluten. A tiny fraction of adults, between 1 and 2 percent, have true (and truly dangerous) food allergies. All human cultures consider fur, paper and hair inappropriate as food.

And that's about it. Everything else is learned. Newborns are not repelled even by the sight and smell of putrefied meat crawling with maggots.

So, Steingarten figured, he would cure himself of his food aversions by exposure: He would eat all of the foods he disliked, eight or 10 times each if necessary, until he no longer had a phobia of them.

After six months, it worked. He no longer had phobias of those foods, and even proclaimed that "kimchi has become my national pickle, too." Steingarten had intentionally acquired what we call "acquired tastes."

Forest asked if I would crew—and maybe also pace, if I was up for it—for him and Canyon in a 100-mile race at the end of April. The race was in Maryland, along the C&O Canal Towpath, the 184-mile multi-use trail from Washington, D.C.'s Georgetown neighborhood to Cumberland, Maryland. The Fontandango 50 still fresh in my mind, I wondered if I could even keep up. Forest assured me that he and Canyon would run together, until he couldn't keep up with Canyon anymore, so by Mile 70, maybe I'd just be pacing him and not Canyon, and that with 70 miles under his belt, he probably wouldn't be moving too quickly. Plus it was flat, or almost as flat as a 100-mile race could be—the course followed a trail on the bank of the Potomac River for the entire time, save about four miles total. OK, sure. I felt sort of in debt to the universe in the crewing and pacing department, having had people show up at all my races and help me out—including Forest, who had paced and filmed as Jayson and I dragged ourselves through the final 30 miles of the Run Rabbit Run 100 last fall.

I flew to D.C. and rented a car, arriving the evening before the race. We were up at 5:30 the next morning, and the runners took off at 7:00 a.m. from Camp Manidokan, a Methodist retreat center perched about 200 vertical feet up a hill from the Potomac. The only significant elevation gain of the race was when the runners came back through the start/finish area at Camp Manidokan at Mile 59, and again at the end at Mile 100.

The elevation profile looked like this:

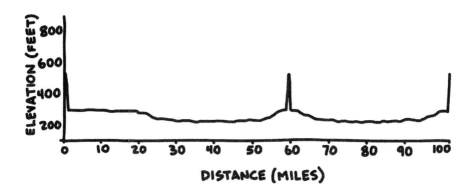

I was to meet the guys with a big duffel bag of their food, clothes, and water at Mile 27.5, Mile 48, and then again at Mile 69.5, at which point I would put on my running shoes and run the rest of the race with them, or at least with Forest. Because the course was a bunch of back-and-forth sections on the C&O Canal, Mile 27.5, Mile 48, and Mile 69.5 were all at the same place, where the C&O Canal trail passed by a commuter train parking lot in Brunswick, Maryland.

Here's a simplified map of the race course:

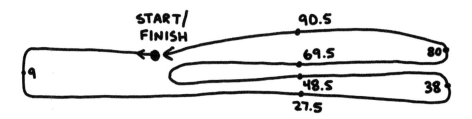

Since all of our rendezvous points were at the same spot, I could have just napped in the car all day, or sat in a lawn chair and read a book. Theoretically, anyway. We didn't have any sort of tracking device, so the only way to estimate what time the guys would be coming through was to guess, using rough math. They could be running 8-minute miles, or maybe they were conserving energy and jogging 12-minute miles. Multiply by 27.5 miles, and they were either going to get there at 10:40 a.m. or 12:30 p.m.

William Goldman wrote the screenplay for the film that would become *Butch Cassidy and the Sundance Kid* in 1969. But when he first tried to sell it around Hollywood, studios didn't want it. One reason: the protagonists spend a huge chunk of the movie trying to get away from the Superposse chasing them, and in American movies, heroes always stay and fight.

From *LIFE* magazine's special issue celebrating the 50th anniversary of the film:

Studios showed no interest in Goldman's screenplay. One executive even scoffed at the idea of filming in South America. When Goldman replied that Butch and Sundance "went there," the studio head said, "All I know is John Wayne don't run away."

In his 2000 memoir *Which Lie Did I Tell? More Adventures in the Screen Trade*[30], Goldman wrote that the middle section of the script—the running part—was the toughest part to write:

My killer problem was that my guys had to do the unthinkable in a western: *run away.*

But the running was one of Goldman's favorite parts of the legend of Butch and Sundance—no historical evidence has been found that Sundance ever killed anyone during the flight to Bolivia depicted in the movie, and Goldman wrote the scene in which Butch admits he's not much for violence himself, when Paul Newman (as Butch) says to Robert Redford, playing Sundance: "Kid there's somethin' I think I oughta tell ya. I never shot anybody before."

Audiences were more than OK with the movie's heroes choosing to run instead of fight. *Butch Cassidy and the Sundance Kid* became the highest-grossing western film ever made.

I waited with Forest and Canyon's parents, Doug and Trish, at the end of the parking lot where the trail passed through. Almost the entire race was along the nearly dead-flat C&O Canal towpath, which was used to pull boats up and down the Cumberland & Ohio Canal from 1831 to 1924, mostly to transport coal from the Allegheny Mountains. The entire canal is 184.5 miles, but the race only used about 30 miles of it, with runners going back and forth on the path, through the tunnel of trees along the canal.

Doug and Trish and I chatted, paced around, looked at our watches, and I scrawled calculations on scraps of paper. The guys came through Mile 27.5 just before noon, looking good. We gave them water and some food, and they discarded some layers, and within a few minutes, the brothers took off down the trail again. We noted the time they left and tried to estimate how long it would take them to run the next 20.5 miles. I figured that even if they picked up their pace a little bit and started cranking out 10-minute miles, we still had at least three hours to kill in the commuter train parking lot in Brunswick, Maryland, which is not someplace I would have ever predicted I'd hang out for an entire day.

Luckily, there was a coffee shop in Brunswick too, just up the hill from the parking lot.

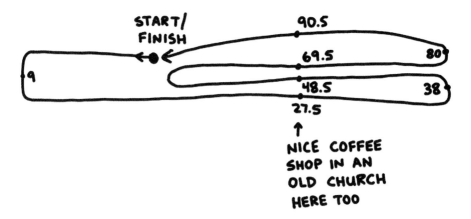

Why is ultrarunning a fringe, obscure sport with almost no fans, while sports like football and mixed martial arts have millions of fans, pack stadiums, and pay star athletes millions of dollars?

Is it because we like violence? I can't begin to count the number of bad guys I've seen killed on screen since I started watching rated-R movies as a teenager (and good guys too). We watch the big hits in football games over and over on replays, and then again on sports highlight shows and on Twitter. We use war metaphors to describe football—kill the quarterback, we must defend this house, et cetera. Every once in a while at a hockey game, a fight breaks out, and the crowd goes wild for it. And of course, mixed martial arts is pure fighting, two people in a ring, one wins, one loses. You can say a runner is "fighting" or "battling" during a race, but it's of course totally a figure of speech.

Another theory: watching ultrarunning is boring. It might be one of the most boring things you can do with your weekend. You spend hours sitting around, watching as people you don't know shuffle by on their personal vision quest, waiting for your particular person to shuffle by, at which point you talk to them for a few minutes, they shuffle away, and then you're back to waiting again.

Also, they serve beer and nachos at football games.

The guys came through again just before 4 p.m., looking a little tired, but still good. Forest said his legs were hurting. He was in dynamite shape from all the mountain running he did—four weeks before the C&O Canal 100, he had attempted to beat the fastest known time of the SCAR Traverse, a 70-mile route across the Great Smoky Mountains with almost 20,000 feet of elevation gain, and finished in a little over 17½ hours. But the C&O Canal was flat, so he was making the same striding motion over and over and over, which was way different. He tried switching into shoes with more cushioning, hoping that would work. After a few quick minutes of filling bottles, discarding food wrappers, filling vests with snacks, and changing socks, they were off again.

By my rough math, and the expectation that they would slow down at least a little bit, it looked more and more like I'd be starting to run with Forest and Canyon just after the sun set, and for several hours in the dark.

They came through again at about 8:15 p.m., 15 minutes after sunset, but a few minutes of waning dusky daylight before we'd have to turn our headlamps on to see the trail in front of us. We jogged along parallel to the Potomac, which popped in and out of the trees. As the stars came out, the riffles in the river glittered under the dark sky.

After a couple miles of running, Forest asked if I could try to keep them going at a 12-minute-mile pace. No problem, I said, looking at my watch, which gave me a readout of the running pace every few seconds. I tried to keep up a bit of conversation as we bobbed along on the trail, hoping to keep morale up. We kept the pace right around 12 minutes for five miles, six miles, seven miles, but as we got within a couple miles of the turnaround at the 80-mile aid station, Forest began to drift back a little bit.

At the aid station, I jumped into the role of adult babysitter, as friends had done for me before, asking What Do You Need, How Do You Feel, and directly telling them, You Need to Eat Something. I grabbed food from volunteers and handed it to Forest and Canyon. Forest went into a vault toilet to use the bathroom and was chilled when he came back. He put on layers, and we started off again. Not far from the aid station, Canyon hugged Forest and said he was going to take off on his own.

It was 10.5 miles back to Brunswick at Mile 90.5, and Canyon got there an hour faster than Forest and I did. We had stopped trying to clock 12-minute miles and were alternating walking and jogging. But we had 9.5 miles left, and we were still moving.

When you have to move into a new house or apartment, you can hire professional movers, or ask some friends to help and offer to feed them pizza afterward. The pizza is not a payment for their sacrifice of half of a Saturday to help haul your stuff across town. Pizza is great, but it is not a repayment. It greases the wheels, but in no way does it equal the effort of someone holding up the other end of a sleeper sofa as you maneuver it up multiple flights of stairs. To balance out the universe, you must return the favor in kind.

Forest's running stride had been severely abbreviated over 90 miles, to a hunched shuffle that made me wonder if it was much faster than walking. He preferred me to be in front of him, setting the pace. I jogged slowly, watching the ground in front of my feet for the light from Forest's headlamp. If it faded too much, he had fallen behind me because I was going too fast for him, so I slowed down. We were walk/running 20-minute miles, in the dark. I scanned the hills above the Potomac for lights, wondering if anyone was awake, and what they were doing while a few idiots with lights on their heads were navigating their own personal hells along the riverside path.

We went through one last aid station, lit up with holiday lights, and I drank a cup of coffee. My legs were fine, comparatively, but my head was getting heavy. It was 3:20 a.m., and I'd been awake for almost 22 hours. We shuffled on, mostly silent.

Charlie Todd started a group called Improv Everywhere in 2001 after he and some friends pulled a prank in a West Village bar, in which Todd, who looks a little bit like musician Ben Folds, pretended to be Ben Folds for the evening. (He didn't play piano and sing; just responded when his friends, posing as strangers, came up to him and asked "Hey, are you Ben Folds from Ben Folds Five?")

Improv Everywhere became famous when video clips of their pranks went viral: A flash mob of 80 people in blue polo shirts and khakis walking into a Manhattan Best Buy store, 200-plus people freezing in place all at once for five straight minutes in the middle of Grand Central Station, and the annual "No Pants Subway Ride," in which dozens of people intermittently boarded subway trains in their underwear, to the confusion of riders going about their everyday commutes.

In 2011, Todd gave a TED Talk titled "The Shared Experience of Absurdity[31]," in which he talked about some people's cynical reactions to the elaborate pranks Improv Everywhere spent so much time and effort creating:

"One of the most common criticisms I see of Improv Everywhere left anonymously on YouTube comments is: 'These people have too much time on their hands.' And you know, not everybody's going to like everything you do, and I've certainly developed a thick skin thanks to Internet comments, but that one's always bothered me, because we don't have too much time on our hands. The participants at Improv Everywhere events have just as much leisure time as any other New Yorkers, they just occasionally choose to spend it in an unusual way.

You know, every Saturday and Sunday, hundreds of thousands of people each fall gather in football stadiums to watch games. And I've never seen anybody comment, looking at a football game, saying, 'All those people in the stands, they have too much time on their hands.' And of course they don't. It's a perfectly wonderful way to spent a weekend afternoon, watching a football game in a stadium. But I think it's also a perfectly valid way to spend an afternoon freezing in place with 200 people in the Grand Central terminal or dressing up like a Ghostbuster and running through the New York Public Library. ...

As kids, we're taught to play. And we're never given a reason why we should play. It's just acceptable that play is a good thing. ... I think, as adults, we need to learn that there's no right or wrong way to play."

If I compared ultrarunning to, say, playing golf, or building model trains, it was a dumber hobby, because it required so much time and effort and in return, produced so much pain.

If you google "Bills Mafia," you might find yourself going down a rabbit hole of articles and videos—but mostly videos—of the antics of fans of the Buffalo Bills. Grown men and women, clad in jerseys with their favorite players' names on the back, drinking, lighting things on fire, injuring themselves with fireworks, and most famously, leaping off the tops of vehicles onto folding tables. These things happen outside the stadium where the Bills play, and arguably have no measurable effect on whether the Bills win or lose.

In early fall 2019, before the Bills started really winning games again, writer John Gonzalez visited the Buffalo tailgate scene on a game day, to bear witness to the Bills Mafia's enthusiasm. In a piece for *The Ringer*, titled "The Unexplainable, Undeniably Entertaining Rituals of the Bills Mafia," Gonzalez wrote[32]:

"It's odd. The whole tailgate scene, obviously, but also the continued fondness for a team that hasn't inspired any real reason for affection in decades. Nostalgia plays a part—both for those who actually experienced Marv Levy's hard-luck, sad-sack, would-be paper champs of the early '90s and those who have only heard the what-if stories. But the years since then have been lean enough that any objective consumers would wonder about the nearly nonexistent return on their substantial comparative emotional and financial investments. At the very least, apathy should have long since set in, rendering Buffalo a northern facsimile of Jacksonville or Miami or wherever it is that the Chargers play. It feels like someone should have called bullshit by now."

You might say that Gonzalez has a point, that all these wild antics are ridiculous for people rooting for a not-so-great team, but you might also ask: wouldn't all that stuff be just as ridiculous if the team was winning?

The real question: Between ultrarunning, and drinking and crashing through tables outside of a football stadium, who has the *real* dumb hobby here?

Most people would say: Both of us.

Maybe it's simply that things have meaning because we decide they have meaning. We stick with something because we believe it will be meaningful, and sometimes it becomes meaningful for no other reason than the fact that we stuck with it.

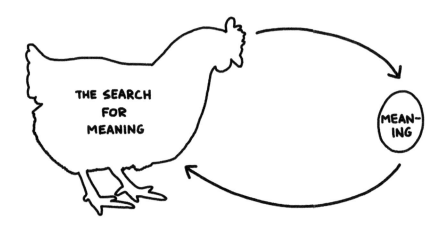

At almost exactly 4:30 a.m., Forest and I came to the turnoff for the last half-mile up the hill to the finish line. After all those miles of the flat canal path, Forest had to hike up some winding singletrack, and hop over a small creek, from rock to rock. I thought, but didn't say, how shitty it would be to slip and fall right here, so close to the finish. He did fine, even jogging the final few hundred feet to the finish line. At that hour, the start/finish atmosphere was grim: a couple people milling around a lonely picnic shelter, ready to cook up a burger for the finishers and their pacers. It was desolate, the kind of scene that might make you a little sad if you weren't so overjoyed to stop running.

Canyon was passed out in the back seat of the car, having somehow put two-plus hours between himself and us in the last 17 or 18 miles. I sat behind the steering wheel and aimed the car toward Brunswick, where we'd pick up my rental car to drive back to the Airbnb to go to sleep. It was a 20-minute drive to Brunswick, and I almost nodded off so many times on the way there that immediately upon arriving, I pulled the car up next to my rental car, put my head against the window and passed out for 45 minutes.

I had no big race, or big running goal, for the rest of the year, which was now my fourth year of ultrarunning, but I kept running. I told myself I didn't want to get out of shape, and that running burned more calories per minute than any other outdoor exercise I did. Both of these things were true. One day in August, though, I started looking online at a 27-mile loop in the Indian Peaks near Denver, crossing the Continental Divide twice, 7,200 feet of elevation gain in total. Hike the uphills, run the downhills and flats. To do it, I would need to filter water. I went to an outdoor gear shop and bought a lightweight squeeze bottle that forced water through a fiber filter, removing bacteria and cysts. I could just stop at a stream or alpine lake, fill the bottle, and squeeze-filter water into my other bottles, and then take off down the trail again.

The trailhead was a 90-minute drive from the house, and I figured I could do the run in six, maybe seven hours, and then drive 90 minutes home. I was not training for anything, and didn't need to do a big day in the mountains to convince myself I was "ready" for something. I just wanted to go move on the trail for a few hours and do something difficult.

A few minutes after cresting the Continental Divide at 11,843-foot Buchanan Pass, after almost three hours of chugging mostly uphill through gradually thinning forest into tundra and then a sea of rock, I started running down the talus on west side of the divide. As I dropped in elevation, the landscape started to go from rock back into tundra and then scraggly trees and bushes, and I picked up speed, my legs gulping big chunks of trail with long strides.

Suddenly, something huge bolted out of some willows to my left, just uphill from the trail. I was moving so fast, not objectively fast, but fast for me, that I was already past it by the time I reacted, my heart leaping into my throat and adrenaline flooding my system. I simultaneously hit the brakes and turned my head to look over my left shoulder to see a moose, running the other direction, away from me.

"Hunters will tell you that a moose is a wily and ferocious forest creature. Nonsense. A moose is a cow drawn by a three-year-old. That's all there is to it. Without doubt, the moose is the most improbable, endearingly hopeless creature ever to live in the wilds. Every bit of it—its spindly legs, its chronically puzzled expression, its comical oven-mitt antlers—looks like some droll evolutionary joke."

—Bill Bryson, *A Walk in the Woods*

Selected facts about moose:

- They are incredibly near-sighted, but almost blind beyond that

- They can weigh up to 1,300 pounds

- They can run up to 35 mph

By the time I hit the trail intersection marking the end of my descent and the beginning of my climb back up to the Continental Divide, it was clear that my "six hours, maybe seven" estimate was going to be off by a little bit. I was well below treeline, having dropped 3,000 feet from Buchanan Pass, and turning left onto my new trail to climb back up, I had 3,700 vertical feet to negotiate up to the second pass.

An hour and a half later, I still had 2,000 feet to go. Six hours, maybe seven, was looking more like eight hours, maybe nine. My feet were starting to fill with micro-aches, and the pins and needles of fatigue were poking my quads and hips, and slowly those aches multiplied as my watch ticked off the miles—which were not going by as quickly as I would have liked. I caught myself listing off the myriad discomforts I was feeling—legs, feet, slight headache, nose running, general tiredness from not sleeping that well last night, maybe a blister forming on the inside of my big toe(s), too-warm water bottles, the evaporation of my day's allotted patience—and I'd make myself look up, take in the alpine scenery, and tell myself, look at that, it's beautiful up here. And that worked for a few minutes at a time.

Humans—or at least some humans—love to eat spicy foods. Other animals, it seems, do not. Psychologist Paul Rozin formally studied chimpanzees in captivity[33], and informally studied dogs in Mexico[34], and found that animals rarely develop a preference for spicy foods. Humans, Rozin set out to prove in a 2013 paper[35], get pleasure from "benign masochism," or hedonic reversals: getting good feelings from things that should make us feel bad, or "enjoying initially negative experiences that the body (brain) falsely interprets as threatening."

Rozin's team of researchers surveyed 390 people, asking them to assign a numerical rating of 0 to 100 in order to rate how much they liked each item on a list of 30 uncomfortable experiences, in eight categories: Sad, Burn, Disgust, Fear, Pain, Alcohol, Exhaust, Bitter, including experiences like watching scary movies, listening to sad music, getting massages, hearing disgusting jokes, eating spicy food, drinking unsweetened coffee, being physically active, and being physically exhausted.

Participants gave the highest ratings to: Feeling physically active, thrill rides, feeling exhausted after physical activity, eating spicy food, and listening to sad music. The lowest scores: flashes of cold pain, and eating stinky cheese, which came in dead last.

I finally popped up over the 12,570-foot pass after what felt like hours of negotiating one million switchbacks. Already seven hours had passed, and I had five and a half miles to run downhill to my car. It was shaping up to be the slowest marathon I'd ever run, if I wanted to call it a marathon.

I took my time moving down the other side of the pass on tired legs, finally picking up the pace a little bit as the trail dropped between alpine lakes, and finally below treeline. Picking my way through the steep, rocky, rooted trail as it descended seemed to be eating up more time than it should, but I reminded myself I didn't care. No one was waiting for me at any finish line, or even at the parking lot. With my water filter and the food I still had in my vest, I could decide to run five more miles if I wanted to, or maybe ten.

But when the trail ended on an asphalt road, with a couple hundred feet to the car, I knew I was done. I looked down at my watch: 26.85 miles. I jogged across the parking lot, and up another trail for a couple hundred feet—might as well make it an even 27 miles, I thought. As the number clicked over, I stopped my watch and walked the last few feet to the car. I sat in the drivers' seat for a few minutes, savoring the feeling of sitting down and letting my legs rest for just a little bit before I finally turned the key into the ignition to start the drive home.

To dig a hole for a fencepost, you need a tool called a posthole digger. It's not an expensive item, maybe $40 for a lower-end one. It looks kind of like a big scissors made of two shovels joined together.

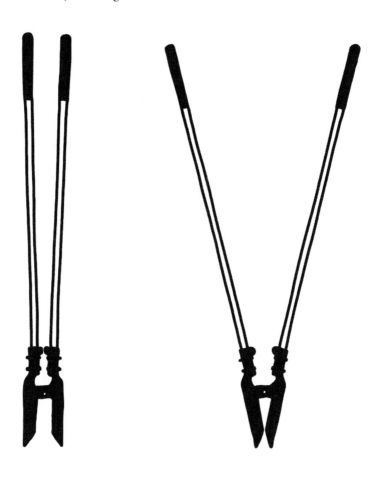

It's simple, but it works: it enables you to dig a hole with parallel sides and lift the dirt out of the bottom of the hole each time you dig down. When you're digging a hole for a fencepost, you need it to be a couple feet deep, so that you're burying two or three feet of an eight-foot-tall fencepost. You want a hole that's basically a perfect cylinder, about three times as wide as your fencepost, so about 12 inches. Which is what you get if you use a $40 posthole digger.

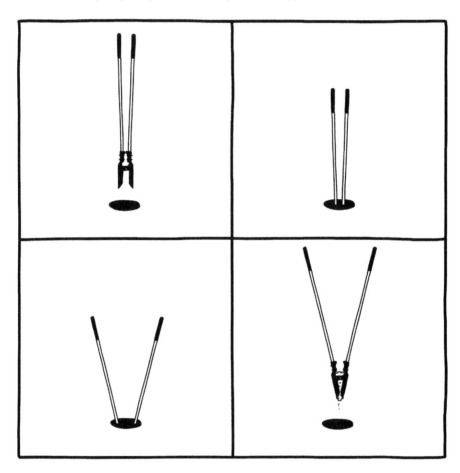

When Hilary and I started to talk in earnest about getting a dog, we noted that we'd need to add a bit of fence to enclose our tiny Denver backyard. So I bought four fenceposts, some concrete, and some panels of wooden fencing. I definitely considered buying a posthole digger, and then talked myself out of it. I mean, $40 for something I'd literally use just this one time? I'd be fine.

A foot or so down into digging the first hole with a shovel, I realized the wisdom of using a posthole digger. It's difficult, if not impossible, to dig a neat, 1-foot diameter, 2-foot-deep cylindrical hole in the ground with a shovel. Still. A trip to buy a posthole digger would take at least 40 minutes round trip, plus the $40, plus the humbling experience of admitting to myself that my previous decision to not purchase a posthole digger was in fact not that smart.

I grabbed a pair of work gloves out of our garage and a small gardening hand trowel, and started to dig the holes by hand, reaching into the bottom of the hole every few seconds to pull dirt and rocks out by hand. It occurred to me at some point that this process might actually be taking me just as much time as I would have spent driving back and forth to buy a posthole digger, if not more time.

But I had committed to this strategy, which was not unlike using a teaspoon instead of a ladle to fill bowls of soup at a dinner party. I settled in and dug the holes, not quickly, but effectively, with my shovel and trowel, and we put the posts in, filled the holes with concrete, and the next day, finished the fence. A few months later, we got a dog. Hilary let me name him Rowlf, after the piano-playing dog in *The Muppet Show*.

I stood in the dark in the desert near Moab, Utah, at 6:25 a.m. on a Saturday at the end of January, waiting for Hilary to hand me her puffy jacket in the final seconds before she ran through the start corral at the beginning of the Arches 50-Mile. In a few minutes, the sun would pop up over the horizon, slowly illuminating the rust-colored sandstone cliffs. The temperature would hover around freezing the whole day, and only some of the snow on the trails and roads would be in danger of softening in the daytime sun.

I was to meet Hilary at the 15.1-mile mark and again at the 44.5-mile mark with some food and a bag full of stuff she might need: new socks, different layers, food, band-aids. The spot was near the Klonzo aid station, at the end of about five miles of dirt road. My biggest worry was that I'd drive down the road in Hilary's Subaru station wagon in the morning, and then the sun would warm and melt so much snow on the road and I'd get stuck trying to drive out again. There were a few other things on my list, such as Hilary slipping on an icy trail, or twisting an ankle, or having gastrointestinal issues, or getting lost, or any of the other things that can go wrong when your spouse is running around the desert for 10 to 12 hours.

With about 90 seconds to go before the start, Hilary passed me her jacket and walked to the back of the pack of 80 or so runners. They took off out of the parking lot, down the bike path paralleling U.S. 191, a swarm of headlamps bobbing along at five or six miles per hour.

I had decided to limit my driving on muddy roads, so instead of driving into the aid station to meet Hilary at Mile 15, then driving out again to eat a civilized lunch in town, I just brought a couple books and figured I'd hang out, enjoying the lack of cell phone signal.

I sat in the car for a while, reading, and as the first runners blazed through the aid station, I started to get restless. Hilary wouldn't be anywhere near the leaders, based on her plan to run conservatively and focus on just finishing her first attempt at the 50-mile distance, but I got out of the car anyway and started to pace around in the dirt. I set up a camp chair off to the side of the aid station, placing all her stuff on it, and my two books.

Runners appeared over a small rise about a half-mile to the south, trickling toward me in loose groups of two or three, switchbacking down the trail as it zigzagged through a broken cliff band. They were too far away to tell if an approaching runner was Hilary or not, so I started walking up the trail a bit, then waiting, then walking closer. There was no reason to; I was just bored and anxious.

Right around the 3-hour mark, she appeared, moving well and looking cautiously optimistic, and not tired at all yet. I took her water bottles and filled them, she grabbed a couple more bits of food, and then I walked with her for a quarter-mile or so down the road to see her off again.

My plan for the day, as crew, broke down like this:

- 6:15 a.m.: Show up at starting line to wait for race to start

- 6:30 a.m.: Watch Hilary run away

- 6:40 a.m.: Drive to Klonzo aid station

- 7:15 a.m.-9:30 a.m.: Wait

- 9:30 a.m.-9:33 a.m.: Make sure Hilary has everything she needs for the next 29.6 miles

- 9:34-a.m.-approximately 4:30 p.m.: Wait

- Approximately 4:30 p.m.-4:33 p.m.: Make sure Hilary has everything she needs for the next 5.2 miles

- Approximately 4:33 p.m.: Drive to finish line

- 5:03 p.m.-approximately 5:30-5:45-ish: Wait at finish line for Hilary to come through

Except at 4:30, there was no Hilary. I paced around in my puffy jacket and muddy running shoes, carrying a book under my arm. I read a few paragraphs here and there, in between scanning the landscape for moving human shapes, which I would then try to wish into the shape of Hilary, which didn't work. At 4:45, no Hilary, 5:00, no Hilary, and then I started to really worry. The cutoff for leaving the Klonzo aid station was at 5:20 p.m.—meaning if you hadn't checked in at 5:20 p.m., your race was over.

At 5:18, I started to walk down the trail toward where I'd been watching runners appear for almost an hour. I was convinced I'd meet someone coming, who would ask, are you Brendan, and then they would tell me Hilary had broken her ankle and was sitting on the trail a couple miles back, or had hit her head on a rock, or something.

At 5:25, Hilary appeared, hiking along just fine. She was OK, but the mud on the course had slowed everyone down—and she had been running with a few other people, and they all walked off the trail at the same point, gone about a half-mile in the wrong direction, maybe three-quarters of a mile, figured it out, gone back the way they came, and gotten back on the course.

You missed the cutoff, I said, so I don't know if they'll let you finish the race now. Maybe you should run the rest of the way to the aid station and see what they say. I took her empty water bottles and ran toward the car. The aid station volunteers had taken down the tent shelter they'd been standing under all day, and had packed up almost everything.

I filled up the water bottles from a gallon jug, then ran over to the aid station, where Hilary was signing her name on a sheet of paper. She had missed the cutoff, but the aid station staff was letting runners continue, as long as they signed a hand-written statement that said she was continuing on her own, was aware of the risks, and was releasing the race organizers from any liability from this point on. I did some quick math.

"You're going to have to put the hammer down," I said, explaining that she had less than an hour to cover 5.2 miles, which, hey, would not be that big of a deal. Except she'd been moving for 11 straight hours so far, it was now dark, and this was the first time she'd ever run more than 31 miles in one stretch, let alone 50 miles. But she headed off into the dark, determined.

I was about to jump into the car and drive to the finish line when I spotted a runner gingerly limping around the aid station. I had seen him earlier—he'd been at the aid station for quite a while, maybe an hour or so. Wondering if he might like a ride to the finish line, I walked up and asked, and yes, he said, that would be great. He had signed up for the 50K race, hadn't trained all that much, and had decided to call it quits here, after just under 26 miles. If I gave him a ride now, he wouldn't have to wait for the aid station volunteers to take him back when they were done.

We got in the car and drove the five miles of dirt road, red-brown mud and slush spraying onto the windshield. We chatted about the race, where we were from, and our jobs. I pulled into the parking lot at the finish line, asked if he had friends or family to give him a ride from here, and he said yes. I dropped him off over by his friends' car and pulled around to find a parking spot.

I grabbed Hilary's puffy jacket, as the temperature was now starting to cool, got out of the car, and walked to the finish line to wait. I was pessimistic about Hilary's fourth-quarter, fourth-down Hail Mary attempt, based on my own experiences of trying to rally for those last five miles when I was exhausted, everything hurt, and 95 percent of me just wanted to lie down. I was projecting my own suckiness at finishing races onto Hilary, yes, but mathematically, it was objectively a longshot.

I chatted up a friend at the finish line for a few minutes, and the guy I'd picked up at the last aid station appeared out of the darkness. He walked up to the volunteers who were handing out finisher medals and said, "I did the 50K, can I get one of those?" and the volunteer handed him a finisher medal.

I tried to not look at my watch or the red numbers ticking by on the race clock above my head, or be sad that Hilary had worked so hard training for this race and was going to miss the cutoff by a few minutes, or alternately, get my hopes up that she'd come sprinting through the finish area with mere seconds to go.

With just under four minutes to go until the race clock clicked over the 12:00:00 mark, a runner appeared about 50 feet from the finish line, moving fast, headlamp bouncing. As the runner got closer, I saw that it was a woman, with blonde hair, wearing the same running vest that Hilary had. When she was 10 feet from the finish line, I realized it was Hilary, who had somehow cranked out 10-minute miles for the final section of the race. I said something like Holy Shit to my friend, and hurried over to meet Hilary. She finished in 11:56:11, a full three minutes and 49 seconds before the cutoff.

In their 1994 book, *Changing the Self: Philosophies, Techniques, and Experiences*[36], authors Thomas M. Brinthaupt and Richard P. Lipka wrote:

Masochists desire pain but eschew injury, and in fact the manuals and workshops that teach people how to engage in sadomasochistic sex uniformly turn out to emphasize advice about how to administer pain without causing injury. Masochists want carefully measured and limited doses of pain, administered by a trusted (and preferably loved) partner, without harm or risk. Some masochists like the illusion of danger or injury, but they do not want to be hurt.

Pain functions thus like a drug to help them escape their normal identities and enter into their scene of sexual play. Regarded as a mild drug, pain can thus be understood as an appealing tool for shrinking the self, particularly in the ego stress pattern. Unlike the calamity pattern, masochists do not seek out a single, intense experience of pain following a particular crisis or setback in their personal lives. Rather, they tend to engage in their sexual activities on a regular or occasional basis (provided they can find a partner, which is often difficult), repeating favorite practices, and gradually moving to more intense or sophisticated patterns. The troubles that go with ego stress vanish from the mind when physical pain is applied. When being whipped, presumably, one's mind does not wander back to deadlines, pressures, long-range problems, financial worries, and other troubles. "A whip is a great way to get someone to be here now," wrote one bisexual woman with ample experience on both sides of sadomasochism. "They can't look away from it, and they can't think about anything else" (Califia, 1983).

On a mild gray day in early March a couple months after Hilary's race, I slammed the door of my car closed a few minutes before 9:00 a.m. and jogged out of the Rooney Road parking lot. I made my way up the asphalt road, across the pedestrian bridge crossing the six lanes of the C-470 freeway, and started hiking up the dirt service road that leads to the top of 6,854-foot Green Mountain. Green Mountain might be more accurately called a mesa, or even a large hill, and it's surrounded by three freeways, a shooting range, a drag racing track, and a motocross park. You can see, but not hear, Red Rocks Amphitheater from the top. It is not pristine wilderness, where wild elk bugle and coyotes roam the washes. It is a chunk of preserved open space on the edge of a city—where I have many times seen elk and heard coyotes.

The dirt road, conveniently, gains 800 feet in about a mile and a half. The 2.2 miles of road from the parking lot to a set of communications towers is not a highly sought-after hike, but it is a stretch of dirt and rocks that you don't have to worry about tearing up when it's snowy and muddy. Green Mountain was where I'd done hundreds of miles of training for my other races, and it felt like I could run most of its trails blindfolded by now. Workers drive trucks on it to service the towers, and the occasional ambulance will ramble up it when a hiker or biker has an accident near the top of the mountain. My next 100-mile race, the Hellbender 100 in the Black Mountains of North Carolina, had 24,000 feet of elevation gain, and I decided to use Green Mountain for my 50-mile training run, which would actually be 52 miles with 12,000 feet of elevation gain.

I had extra socks, extra shoes, extra layers, water, and food in the car. In 50 miles, I would burn somewhere between 8,000 and 10,000 calories, so I had stacks of CLIF BLOKS and Honey Stinger waffles, as well as a few bags of smashed-up Kettle Chips, to pour into my mouth in 200-calorie increments as I hiked.

I had done a charity climb of Mt. Whitney a few years back (with Forest), and over four days, I had noticed that one of the mountain guides on the trip, Chris Werner, seemed to be eating pizza, every day. I asked him about it on the third day, and he told me: After years of working as a mountain guide, he got sick of eating energy bars all the time on these climbs, so every time he had a climb coming up, the night before, he would bake a frozen pizza, cut it into eight slices, put it in a big zip-lock freezer bag, and then shove it into his backpack. And then every day, he could eat cold pizza.

I started doing the same thing for my long runs: I would buy two small vegan frozen pizzas (figuring a lot of cheese would be difficult to digest while running all day), bake them the night before, cut them in half, fold the halves in half, and put them in plastic bags. This gave me four very handy pizza quesadillas, 430 calories each, that I could carry and munch on while walking away from my car.

I hiked up the road, jogging a few of the less-steep sections, then running the flats and downhills. I ran across the top of the mountain and then along the bases of the communications towers, the full sprawl of Denver and its surrounding suburbs in a 180-degree view in front of me. I turned around at the towers and started jogging back the 2.2 miles I had come up, totaling 4.4 miles and about 900 feet of elevation gain. I ran down the road, got to the pedestrian bridge at the other side, and turned around to hike up what I'd just come down. Next lap, I'd just go to the summit of the mountain, skipping the flat running to the communications towers, and make a shorter, steeper lap. This was my plan, which in theory would keep it from getting too monotonous. With almost every other trail covered in snow or muddy, this was my best option.

When I started researching ultramarathon training and running, I found information everywhere on training plans, shoes, gear, hydration, nutrition, and injuries. There's much less information out there about how to avoid boredom.

Despite knowing that the concept of "multitasking" has been thoroughly debunked, I spend most of my work days flitting back and forth from a word processing program, a drawing app, my email, social media accounts, news articles, text messages, and vast quantities of coffee that ensure I will have to get up from my desk to use the bathroom four or five times before noon. Even though I know this is a terrible way to work, I do it. And then, for a hobby, I picked up long-distance running, which required me to do one thing and one thing only for two, three, five, seven hours at a time. I put my phone on airplane mode so I wouldn't get interrupted with text messages or other notifications, and refused to listen to music or podcasts, to fully commit to doing the one thing. I choose to believe that it was not boring, but refreshing—to get away from all the digital crap I gorged on daily.

The "four horsemen of boredom," or four telltale signs that we are experiencing boredom, as defined by psychology professors James Danckert and John D. Eastwood in their 2020 book *Out of My Skull: The Psychology of Boredom*[37], are:

1. Time drags on

2. We struggle to concentrate

3. What we are doing feels pointless

4. A combination of lethargy and restlessness

Perhaps not coincidentally, the four telltale signs that I am running more than, say, 10 miles, are:

1. Time drags on

2. I struggle to concentrate

3. What I am doing feels pointless

4. A combination of lethargy and restlessness, and also my feet and legs hurt

I alternated laps, up and down Green Mountain, up to the towers and back down, up to the summit and back down, repeat. I carried lightweight carbon trekking poles, stretching them in front of me on the uphills, telling myself it was "four-wheel drive," but pretty sure it was mostly just helping me keep my posture upright. On the flats and the downhills, I slipped the wrist straps off, slid my hands down to about the halfway mark on the poles, and ran, carrying them parallel to the ground as I plodded along.

All in all, I would go to the top ridge of the mountain and back 14 times in just under 13 hours. The landscape stayed the same, of course, but the scenery changed by the hour, as the sun rolled across the sky from east to west. Every once in a while, a new hiker or runner would appear, and the cast kept changing throughout the day. On my second lap, I ran downhill on the west side of the mountain and saw Jayson's car in the parking lot. He met me at the pedestrian bridge and ran and hiked with me for 26.5 miles, heading home at about 5:30, at the start of my 11th lap, which left me alone in my own head for the last four laps. I calculated that I'd be doing the last two laps in total darkness.

In *Out of My Skull*, Danckert and Eastwood make a case for some potential "opposites of boredom," including the idea of the state of "flow," a concept developed by psychologist Mihaly Csikszentmihalyi starting in the 1970s. Danckert and Eastwood write:

Although they do not always parse them in exactly the same way, researchers have consistently identified a number of necessary characteristics for flow:

- *our skills and abilities must be up to the challenge;*

- *we need a heightened sense of control;*

- *we need well-defined goals and clear feedback on progress;*

- *our attention must be intensely focused;*

- *our awareness must be so tightly linked to what we are doing that we lose sight of ourselves;*

- *whatever we are doing must feel effortless;*

- *what we do, we do for its own sake—we are intrinsically motivated, and*

- *our sense of time becomes distorted.*

I hadn't gotten very deep into analyzing my mental state while running for long periods of time—but I had noticed one thing: When I felt bad, sad, down in the dumps, or like whatever I was doing was completely pointless and I should just quit, I found that I was usually on an uphill section of trail. When the uphill grade changed to downhill, or just flat, my mood improved. When I was moving along flats or downhill trails, I often felt like a freight train, not necessarily speedy, but unstoppable. I became less concerned about time or how long I was taking, and rarely looked at my watch.

It wasn't necessarily a one-to-one correlation, but the uphill parts generally made me feel bored, and if I found myself in a flow state as defined by Mihaly Csik-szentmihalyi, it was usually when I was on a non-uphill section. It wasn't all flow, but big chunks of time during my long runs certainly were.

I'm not a psychologist, but I might humbly suggest that the difference between a state of boredom and a state of flow is: In a flow state, you give a fuck about what you're doing, and in a state of boredom, you do not. In a flow state, what you're doing is important. Or at least you've tricked yourself into believing it's important.

In 1988 Diane Van Deren was 28, three weeks pregnant with her third child, when she had a grand mal seizure. She was in the passenger seat of a car, reaching into the glove box, and the next thing she knew, she was in a hospital bed. After an MRI, a doctor told her she had epilepsy. A childhood fever had apparently caused her to have a seizure, which damaged part of her brain. But then she went two and a half decades without another seizure, until that day riding around with her mother.

For nearly a decade, she dealt with more seizures and tried almost everything to prevent them—this medication, that medication, diets—and nothing worked. Besides running. Before a seizure began, she noticed she'd feel a tingling sensation all over her body. After a while, she realized that if she put on her running shoes and headed out the door on a run quickly following the strange tingling, she could prevent the seizure from happening. So she ran, out in the woods by her house near Castle Rock, Colorado, for longer and longer stretches, sometimes up to six hours. It worked, until it stopped working, and the seizures came back. Eventually, she was having three to five seizures a week. She was worried that one of the seizures would eventually kill her.

Her doctors told her that sometimes, if the part of the brain where seizures occur can be identified, it might be possible to remove it to prevent future seizures. She said great, let's figure it out. In the hospital, doctors wired electrodes to her brain, and for once, they hoped she'd have a seizure, so they could map where it was happening. It worked.

She had a right temporal lobectomy, a surgery removing a golf-ball-sized chunk of her brain. The seizures disappeared. But so did her ability to read maps. And some of her short-term memory, and organizational skills, and time management. She could never remember where she'd parked her car.

On a whim, she signed up for a 50-mile race she'd read about in a magazine. She won. She signed up for the 100-mile Bighorn Trail Race in Wyoming, and placed. From there, she started racing, a lot, and winning races, becoming a sponsored endurance athlete.

Dr. Donald Gerber, Van Deren's neuropsychologist, says her surgery changed her brain so that she interprets pain differently—that her emotional reaction to pain isn't the same as other people's. And she processes time differently than other runners, who are aware of how long they've been running and how their body should feel based on how long they've been going. Van Deren doesn't have an idea of how tired her legs should be, whether she's been running for an hour or 10 hours. "It's a mental state," Gerber says. "You become enmeshed in what you're doing. It's almost Zen. She can run for hours and not know how long she's been going[38]."

As Van Deren told Radiolab's Mark Phillips in 2011[39], "If I had to say I have an advantage over the other athletes, would be time. Time—I can really get lost in time. ... I stay in the moment."

On my way hiking uphill Green Mountain, I passed a guy in his late 20s or early 30s heading onto a different trail, and we exchanged a quick hello. As I headed across the top, I saw him again, from a distance, and then made my way back downhill. I headed up to do Lap 12, and back down again, as the sun was dropping close to the horizon. As I approached my turnaround point at the end of my 12th lap, I ran into the guy again, and he waved and asked, "What are you training for?"

"Something way worse," I said, saying the thing that had been at the front of my mind all day, and that was keeping me going as I entered my 10th hour of going up and down the same hill.

Well, everybody does something, usually anyway.

In the ancient Greek myth, Hades punishes Sisyphus for twice cheating death by making him roll a boulder up a steep hill, reaching the top only to have the boulder roll down to the bottom again, for eternity. For centuries since, we have referred to pointless, repetitive tasks as "Sisyphean." Although I suppose the only thing separating my hill climbing, or someone's weightlifting, from Sisyphus, is the eternity thing. If humans could live forever, we might be able to exercise forever, and would we be surprised if someone repackaged the myth of Sisyphus as "The Sisyphus Workout"?

Eastbound & Down, Season 1, Episode 1:

Former professional baseball player Kenny Powers returns to his hometown in Shelby County, North Carolina, to take a job as a substitute teacher at Jefferson Davis Middle School. On his first day back, the school principal, Terrence Cutler, welcomes him, and jovially tries to find a little bit common ground.

Terrence: There's something you need to know about, Kenny. You're not the only athlete here at Jeff Davis. I happen to be training for a triathlon right now. Doing a lot of running, cycling, swimming—you know all about that.

Kenny: No, actually, I don't. I play real sports. Not trying to be the best at exercising.

Green Mountain is probably nobody's favorite summit in Colorado. It's not even the most popular Green Mountain in a 30-mile radius—the Green Mountain on Boulder's western edge is steeper, more scenic, and way more famous.

But when you climb up from the base of my Green Mountain, the less-famous one, on the west side at night, this happens: you put some distance and elevation between you and the C-470 freeway, turn a few corners as the dirt road winds up a gully, and probably once out of five times in the fall and early winter, you'll see elk to one side or another as you hike up in the dark, and after about a mile and a half, the road rolls over the top, and you have a view of the top of the mesa in front of you, and the lights of all of Denver and its suburbs spreading across the plains below, and it's such a flood of light that you can barely see any stars above, and you can't separate the 50-story buildings downtown from anything else, but maybe if the Broncos or Rockies are playing a game you can make out the stadium, and a cynic might be a little dismayed by the urban sprawl, but I try to be a bit more of a realist and just appreciate that nobody's built condos on top of Green Mountain, and that I can come up here and have the place to myself in the dark for a few minutes, and isn't it great that I can see the lights of three million people right there but it's so dark up here I have to use a headlamp to see the rocky road in front of me, and it's so quiet I can hear my breath as I run downhill toward the towers for the 14th and last time today, which means I'm done, and I'm too tired to worry anymore today about the 100-mile race I have coming up, and isn't it great that once I turn my back on the city lights to head down the other side, it means I only have 2.4 miles back to my car and I can finally go home?

One Monday night in Denver, Hilary and I sat at a table at the jazz jam at the Meadowlark Bar, and I fixated on the drummer in a four-piece band: a youngish man who was in absolute command of the drum set. He never looked at where his sticks landed—only at the bass player, guitar player, or trumpet player. Awed and a little envious, I wondered how he got that good, and how long it took him for the drum set to become an extension of his body. Probably hours of playing every week, for years. I imagined dedicating myself to something so fully, and having that much fun with it. If you could play an instrument, you wouldn't even have to speak the same language as other musicians. Anywhere in the world, you could just sit down and jam.

I thought back to eighth grade, when I had moved to a new town, and after having played in the marching band at my last school, I'd figured I'd be able to continue at my new school. But they already had enough snare drummers for the marching band, and I didn't want to play the much less sexy bass drum. Plus I wanted to play football in high school, and eventually, I'd have to choose between the two, because the marching band played at halftime of football games, and nobody could do both. In my hometown, like probably a lot of American towns back then, athletes were heroes. Band kids were, well, less celebrated. So I chose football, even though I was small and not particularly talented.

I caught a touchdown pass the next fall, during the season our freshman football team technically went undefeated, with one tie. It would be the only touchdown I ever scored in an official game. Eventually, we sold my snare drum to a music shop a few towns over, and I unintentionally resigned myself to being a music fan, instead of a player.

A few decades after my snare drum found a new home, I picked up Susan Cain's book *Quiet: The Power of Introverts in a World That Can't Stop Talking*. As a lifelong extrovert, I was a bit shocked as the book gradually made obvious to me that I was not, in fact, a lifelong extrovert. I had prided myself on being able to strike up a conversation with almost anyone, able to find something in common with anyone I sat next to on a plane, people I met at parties, even convenience store clerks if they were feeling chatty. I had been a bartender and a waiter for four years, and those are not jobs for introverts. I had played team sports all through junior high and high school.

In *Quiet*, Susan Cain writes about Dale Carnegie's early-1900s rise to fame as a public-speaking icon, and how his success in part spread the idea of the Extrovert Ideal[40]:

Carnegie's journey reflected a cultural evolution that reached a tipping point around the turn of the twentieth century, changing forever who we are and whom we admire, how we act at job interviews and what we look for in an employee, how we court our mates and raise our children. America had shifted from what the influential cultural historian Warren Susman called a Culture of Character to a Culture of Personality.

As the country's ideal shifted, Cain wrote, we began to value gregariousness and charisma in adults, and started to worry about quiet kids with solitary hobbies, instead urging them to be more social, because it would help them fare better as adults:

When these children grew older and applied to college and later for their first jobs, they faced the same standards of gregariousness. University admissions officers looked not for the most exceptional candidates, but for the most extroverted. Harvard's provost Paul Buck declared in the late 1940s that Harvard should reject the "sensitive, neurotic" type and the "intellectually over-stimulated" in favor of boys of the "healthy extrovert kind." In 1950, Yale's president, Alfred Whitney Griswold, declared that the ideal Yalie was not a "beetle-browed, highly specialized intellectual, but a well-rounded man." Another dean told [William H.] Whyte that "in screening applications from secondary schools he felt it was only common sense to take into account not only what the college wanted, but what, four years later, corporations' recruiters would want. 'They like a pretty gregarious, active type,' he said. 'So we find that the best man is the one who's had an 80 or 85 average in school and plenty of extracurricular activity. We see little use for the "brilliant" introvert.'"

It's not like you check a box on a form in high school and make a choice between trying to be an All-American Extrovert Athlete or trying to be a Not-So-All-American Band/Art/Book Geek, but you do make choices. By the time I bought my first Kurt Cobain T-shirt, I had already quit band in favor of the football team, which was a very un-Kurt Cobain thing to do. I can't say what I was thinking at the time, but it was probably along the lines of "girls/people like athletes," which is of course a dumb way to make choices in your life, but when I was 14 years old, I wasn't making a lot of smart choices.

Even before I read *Quiet*, a more perceptive me might have noticed that I was starting to prefer running by myself, for hours at a time. If a friend suggested we run together, I would say yes, and it would always be fun, but what really felt good was an hour or five on a trail by myself, in my own head, exchanging only a handful of words with the few people I'd encounter on the trail before getting back to the free jazz of my thoughts, jamming along with the rhythm of my running shoes bouncing off the dirt and rocks.

At the Hellbender 100 starting line near Black Mountain, North Carolina, at 4:30 a.m., lots of runners had trekking poles. Most were collapsed and folded up, strapped into vests or race belts, stowed away for the first 4.5 miles, which we'd run on asphalt highways, with flashing lights clipped to each of our 80 vests in case a car came along during the wee hours of the morning.

My plan was to start slow, to not get carried away by the energy of the pack, so I milled around at the back of the pack until the official start, and then jogged through the starting arch dead last, fumbling to start my watch as I passed underneath it. On the highway, my conservative pace put me in earshot of a loose group of guys and their intermittent chatter. Some of it was nervous, some self-deprecating to mask nervousness, a tone which I identified with, and some a combination of self-deprecating and confident, which I also identified with. The blend was a style of talking that communicates you've done this kind of thing before and you have an idea of how it's going to go for you, and that you have no illusions that you will finish in the top 25, or top 50.

Like the Run Rabbit Run, the Hellbender was also 100 miles. But it had 4,000 feet more elevation gain, for a total of 24,000 feet. The elevation profile looked like this:

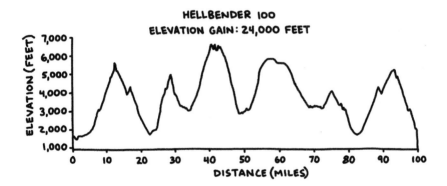

When I had been training for the Run Rabbit Run, someone told me about a friend of theirs who, like me, had tried to train for their first 100-mile race by the book. They'd put in a ton of miles, with many, many long runs. The friend had done just fine at their first 100-miler, but for their next 100-miler, they didn't put in nearly as many training miles, and their longest training run was something like 30 miles. And they finished their second 100-mile race just fine.

This was not advice from a running coach, or a scientific study—it was purely anecdotal evidence of Some Guy who I heard about secondhand. But I had arrived at the starting line of the Run Rabbit Run feeling pretty beat-down after running a bajillion training miles, so maybe Some Guy was onto something? This time, I'd kept my weekly total around 40 miles, and still did my Sisyphean 52-mile day on Green Mountain, but overall, I ran a little less, and felt a little better. Which is not to say I had cured my anxiety about the Hellbender 100.

If a person who lived in the western United States were to strut into the pre-race check-in at an event like the Hellbender 100, looking down their nose (literally or metaphorically) at the lower-elevation mountains on the East Coast, believing they would have no trouble at all flying up and down the less-rocky peaks of the Appalachian Mountains for 100 miles in a not-yet-very-famous ultramarathon race, I might advise that person to check their ego at the door, as the saying goes.

I was not that person. But I did completely forget about the general lack of switchbacks on trails in the eastern United States, compared to the trails of the West, where I had spent about 99% of my hiking and running time up until that point.

A rough comparison:

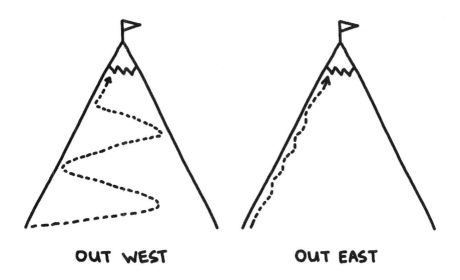

OUT WEST   **OUT EAST**

Also, when the race organizers allot you 40 hours to finish a 100-mile race, it's not because they love hanging out at the finish line waiting for runners. It's because they know they have designed a very difficult race course, and there's a solid chance that it might take a reasonably fit person 39 hours, 59 minutes, and 59 seconds to reach the finish line.

Did my training run going up and down the dirt road on Green Mountain for 13 straight hours help? I felt pretty good for the first 50 miles of the Hellbender. The singletrack trails felt bumpy and rocky, with tight turns and steep steps, making it hard to run very fast downhill. Rain poured on us for an hour straight in the early morning as we climbed up toward the Blue Ridge Parkway. I hiked and jogged for a while with a guy from Maryland named Mike, and as the pack started to spread out, I got out a little ahead of Mike and found myself on my own.

Just before the five-hour mark, I hit 20 miles and resisted doing math in my head that would tell me that 100 miles at 4 mph = 25 hours. I knew there was no way I'd cover the last 25 miles as fast as the first 25 miles, but still, every minute counted, and I let gravity carry me down a wide dirt road for the next few miles, clicking off three sub-8-minute miles in a row. I tried to hurry through aid stations, just filling my water bottles and grabbing a little food to shove down as I walked away, hoping to minimize my time moving zero mph.

When I got to the Neals Creek aid station at Mile 32.8, I was running downhill, feeling good, maybe even fast. Hilary and Forest were waiting with the back hatch of the rental car open, equipped with cold pizza and an Americano. I drank a few sips of the coffee while refilling bottles and running snacks. I resisted sitting down, and hiked away smashing half a vegan pizza into my mouth while offering some to Forest, who had decided to accompany me to the summit of Mt. Mitchell, seven miles away and 3,500 feet up.

The final few hundred feet to the top of Mt. Mitchell are on a paved path, leading from a parking lot to the summit. At 6,684 feet, Mt. Mitchell is the highest point east of the Mississippi River, the tallest of the Appalachian Mountains, all but the very top covered in spruce and fir forest. You can drive almost all the way to the summit, save for the short walk to the top of the observation deck. At the top, I sort of felt like I should enjoy the view a little bit, especially when Forest pointed out that we were quite lucky to have a clear view in all directions. But the clock was ticking, so I took off after a few seconds and a quick photo. Forest saw me off from the 40-mile aid station, and I started heading through the forest across Mt. Mitchell's north ridge, on my way to cross the next few summits: Mt. Craig, Balsam Cone, Cattail Peak, and Potato Hill.

I had a burrito in my hand and was happily munching away as I strode along the singletrack when I realized I had to poop, and fairly immediately. Pooping, of course, being another activity that requires use of the hands, and, in the middle of the woods, puts one in danger of violating the "don't shit where you eat" maxim, because you really want your hands to be as clean as possible when you eat, especially when poop is involved, especially when hand-held food is also involved.

Two miles back, I could have sat down on a toilet, done my thing, and used some hand sanitizer afterward. Alas.

Over the years, I have carried small bottles of hand sanitizer with me in the back-country, and in situations where I didn't have hand sanitizer, I might take a couple big drinks from my water bottle and gradually spit the water onto my hands while scrubbing, or try to rinse my hands in a creek before I next touched food. But in the year before the Hellbender 100, I had started using a new technique that I developed based on a friend's strategy for changing tampons while she was rock climbing. I carried a single wet wipe and a latex glove in my running vest, and if the need arose, I did this:

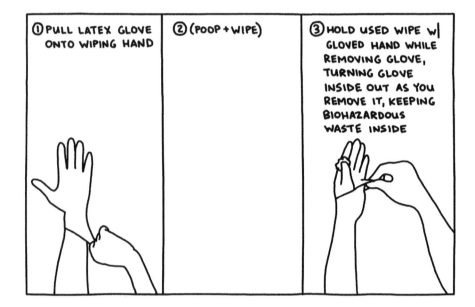

I had really wanted to get to the Colbert Creek aid station at Mile 48 before dark, and I almost did, arriving at 8:20 p.m., having begrudgingly clicked my headlamp on for the last few minutes. Hilary helped me fill my bottles, re-pack energy blocks and waffles into my vest, and walked me down a road to the singletrack I'd climb to the Buncombe Horse Trail. When she turned around, she would walk back to the rental car, drive it to the Neals Creek aid station at Mile 71.5, where she would roll out a sleeping bag and try to get a few hours of sleep before joining me for the final 28 miles to the finish line.

I headed up the now pitch-black trail for my next 3,000-foot climb, totally alone for over an hour, with no visible lights anywhere. With 80 runners spread out on a 100-mile race course, at Mile 50, there could be as much as nine or 10 hours between the first-place runner and the last-place runner, and I was not surprised to be totally by myself. I kept my headlamp on a low-beam setting to conserve the battery, head pointing down at the trail, and every once in a while, a small flag appeared to let me know I was still on the race course.

Finally, I caught up to a few headlamps, climbing up the hill above me. I slowly gained on a runner, and eventually passed him, hiking uphill just a tiny bit faster. We said our hellos, and he said, "That next aid station's gotta be coming up soon, doesn't it?" Which was a thought I had been trying to keep out of my head the entire day. Better, I thought, to just settle into the grind and be pleasantly surprised when an aid station appeared than to keep looking at my watch and wishing for that visible sign of progress.

Of course, I knew I would be saying, or at least thinking, the same thing at some point. But I was trying to put it off as long as possible.

For the final six weeks of the summer before my first semester in college, I got a job working third shift at a factory in my hometown. It was an abrupt shift from my dishwashing and busboy job at a restaurant on the other side of town, where even though the work was hard and sometimes felt unending, I could always chat a little bit with the friends I worked with, even when we were slammed with a 200-person wedding party.

At the factory, I worked 11 p.m. to 7 a.m., operating a hydraulic press. I was required to wear eye protection, earplugs, steel-toed boots, jeans, a denim shirt, and gloves at all times. The job was very simple: clock in at 10:55, put my lunch in the break room fridge, and go stand in front of the press. Parts rolled off a conveyor belt with excess metal around them, and I would grab them with my left hand, situate them properly inside the press, pull two levers on the front of the machine, one in each hand, and watch the press come down and cut away the excess metal. When the press went back up, I would grab the parts and toss them into appropriate bins, and pull the waste metal out and throw that into a different bin.

I did this for two hours, until my 15-minute break. Then I'd work another hour and 45 minutes until my 30-minute lunch break. Then another hour and a half until my last 15-minute break, and then another hour and 45 minutes until the first-shift people showed up and relieved me. There was one other guy working in the room with me, and we'd chat a little bit, exchanging maybe 100 words every shift. We were not allowed to listen to music, just the chugging drone of industrial machinery. The conveyor belt never stopped, unless we changed what type of part we were punching out. Sometimes I'd spend three hours punching two parts—for example, the levers of an RV door handle, and the housing for the same door handle. The piece that came through on the conveyor belt might look like this:

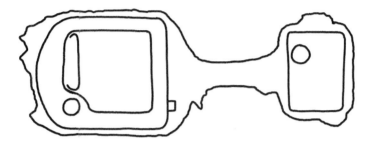

After I punched out the two parts, they looked like this:

All the pieces went to another room in the factory, where they'd be assembled by another group of workers, and then those parts would be shipped somewhere to be installed on an RV or a tractor somewhere.

There were no windows, but it was dark outside for all but a few minutes at the end of the shift anyway. There was no way to tell if time was passing, aside from looking at the clock, which I tried to avoid as much as possible. I stood in front of the press, turned to my left, grabbed metal off the line, put it in the press, pulled the handles, cleaned out the parts and the junk metal, then turned back to my left to grab the next bit coming down the line.

Then, I turned to my left, grabbed metal off the line, put it in the press, pulled the handles, cleaned out the parts and the junk metal, then turned back to my left to grab the next bit coming down the line.

And then, I turned to my left, grabbed metal off the line, put it in the press, pulled the handles, cleaned out the parts and the junk metal, then turned back to my left to grab the next bit coming down the line.

Eventually I'd get my break, and then I'd go back to work, and at some point my shift would end, and I'd clock out and walk to my car and drive home in the early morning light.

German-American psychologist Hugo Münsterberg's writings in the early 1900s made him more or less the father of something that would later be called "industrial psychology," or the study of human behavior as it pertains to work. Münsterberg was interested in using psychology to help figure out how to match people's personalities and abilities to appropriate jobs, and he believed that would help pretty much everything: performance, productivity, career longevity, and motivation.

As part of his research, Münsterberg visited large factories, and one of the things he liked to do during his factory visits was to find the person that he thought had the most boring job, and ask them how they felt about the job. He assumed that people who performed repetitive tasks every day for years and years would find them tedious and unenjoyable.

In two examples in his 1913 book *Psychology and Industrial Efficiency*[41], he was pleasantly surprised that repetitive labor was not, as he'd thought, "a source of discomfort" for workers: A woman who was responsible for packing 13,000 incandescent bulbs in tissue paper every day, adding up to approximately 50,000,000 bulbs in her 12-year career, packing a box of 25 lamps every 42 or 43 seconds, told Münsterberg that she found the work "really interesting," and that she felt there was "continuous variation," in that she always managed to find "something to observe and something to think about." At another factory, Münsterberg interviewed a man whose job was to feed a machine that punched a precisely-placed hole in metal strips, which required the man to perform about 34,000 uniform movements every day on the job for 14 years. The man told Münsterberg that he found the work interesting and stimulating, and that he actually found himself liking the work more than he had at the beginning of his career. The man seemed to enjoy that his job required total concentration, and, Münsterberg wrote, "he added especially that it is not only the wage which satisfies him, but that he takes decided pleasure in the activity itself."

Münsterberg wrote that he did happen upon many people who had, it seemed to him, more interesting and varied factory jobs, but who "complained bitterly over the monotonous, tiresome factory labor."

He concluded: "I became more and more convinced that the feeling of monotony depends much less upon the particular kind of work than upon the special disposition of the individual. It cannot be denied that the same contrast exists in the higher classes of work."

During the holiday break my first year in college, I went back to the factory to work nights again, this time on the assembly line. It was not actually a "line": I sat with a group of women and one other guy at a table, with several boxes of parts in the middle of the table, and we assembled the parts by hand. We were each required to meet quotas, for example, a certain number of padlocks produced in 45 minutes, or a certain number of door handles assembled in an hour. I worked as fast as I could, and every time we finished our group quota of a certain part, I reported my count to my supervisor and watched her write it on her sheet. I don't think I made a single individual quota during the three and a half weeks I worked there, despite my frantic efforts. But no one talked shit to me—I assume having someone really slow jump in and help during the holidays was better than nothing, like having a group of people rowing a boat, and even though one has a broken arm, having them at least pull an oar with their good arm helps a little bit over the course of a long trip.

At the end of my holiday break, I clocked out and got to go back to college. The women I worked with on the assembly line kept clocking in every night at 11 p.m. and cranking out parts for months or years.

I told myself I wanted to try the Hellbender 100 because it was a challenging new experience, and because I just generally assume that by doing hard things, I will acquire new knowledge, or even wisdom. In the best-case scenario, I will go through something that leads to a lesson, which I can then apply to life. My hope, of course, is that that lesson is lofty, borderline mystical or even spiritual, a lesson I will carry with me for decades, and maybe even share with other people—real Hero's Journey shit, if you will.

I eventually got to the top of the climb at about Mile 55 and the course turned onto the Buncombe Horse Trail, which was a flat-ish to slightly downhill grade for almost five miles. Which would have been nice, but the entire trail was basically a shelf of water, saturated in spots and turned to puddles in others. At first, I tried to hop between the dry-ish spots, but quickly realized the futility of that—and how much precious energy it would take. I gave up and began running straight through the water, soaking my shoes and socks. I figured I could handle having wet feet for however far I had to go to the 71-mile aid station where I'd see Hilary and be able to change socks, no big deal.

I first saw the famous ultrarunning movie *Forrest Gump* in a Charles City, Iowa, theater during my freshman year in high school, which was the nearest town that had a movie theater. By the time the Hellbender 100 rolled around, I had forgotten the part where Lieutenant Daniel Taylor says this to Forrest Gump and Benjamin Buford "Bubba" Blue:

"There is one item of G.I. gear that can be the difference between a live grunt and a dead grunt. Socks, cushion, sole, O.D. green. Try and keep your feet dry when we're out humpin'. I want you boys to remember to change your socks wherever we stop. The Mekong will eat a grunt's feet right off his legs."

The moisture started causing blisters almost immediately, on the bottoms of both my feet, just past where my toes joined the balls of my feet. I couldn't see this, but I could feel it. I didn't really need visual confirmation, because I could do nothing to help the situation. A couple blisters, no big deal. At the Mile 65 aid station, I grabbed a couple avocado rolls and some boiled potatoes sitting next to a mountain of salt, then forced myself to run the downhill, six miles to go to new socks.

My legs hurt, my feet were starting to really hurt, and the pain from the blisters was increasing. I had figured that the blisters would form and then cause a little pain, which would remain at the same level until the blisters popped, no big deal.

With three miles to go until the aid station, I started to feel sad, and sorry for myself, and just didn't want to run anymore. What was wrong? I reveled in some self-pity for a couple minutes and then realized: I haven't had any caffeine in a long time. I popped a package of caffeinated CLIF BLOKS out of my vest pocket, shoved three of them in my mouth, and kept hiking, waiting for a lightning bolt of good feelings to blast into my brain.

I did not get the lightning bolt. More like a gentle pat on the back, which was enough to get me to drag my legs into a slow jog, which sped up a little bit as I started to see faint lights in the valley below, which was definitely the aid station.

Hilary was waiting for me a few hundred feet up the trail from the car, scanning the few-and-far-between runners trickling in with her headlamp. I made sure I was running all the way in, telling myself I was feeling strong, sort of a way of lying inside my head and recruiting my arms and legs for the misinformation campaign. I stopped and checked in with a volunteer, verifying my race number, and also trying to keep a straight face when I asked, "How far am I behind the lead runners?"

He did not laugh or smile. He just nodded, in the habit of a person who is also fluent in sarcasm when they recognize an attempt at humor, and said, "Well, they finished two and a half hours ago, so …"

"Damn," I said, trying to feign disappointment. "Well, OK then."

Hilary and I walked to the car and I tried to be quick about refilling water and food and changing my socks, but it felt so good to sit down in a camp chair for just a minute. Or two. Or three. Any longer and my will to finish would quickly drip to zero.

I started walking up the road, leaving the aid station, and Hilary moved the car a few hundred yards, leaving the key in the wheel well for Tommy and Abby, our friends who graciously offered to move the car from the aid station to the finish line so that Hilary could pace me for the last 28.5 miles.

I was still munching my vegan half-pizza when Hilary caught me on the road. I mumbled something about the rest of the race being a lot of walking, but please make me jog as much as possible, thank you.

By Mile 74, the pain from my blisters had not subsided, or even stabilized—it was now shooting up into my legs every time I took a step. I tried gritting my teeth, I tried breathing more deeply. I tried, as a competitive kayaker had told me a few years ago, to imagine chewing on the pain and swallowing it. None of these things worked. What would work, I knew, was stopping, sitting down, quitting the race, going back to our Airbnb, popping the blisters, taking a shower, eating a pizza, and sleeping for 12 hours.

And then getting on a plane, flying home, arriving, taking all my running gear, setting it on fire in a steel barrel somewhere, never running again, taking up chess or macrame or something that didn't promise long hours of diverse types of pain as a meaningful experience, living the rest of my life with relative peace and all 10 of my toenails, and retiring somewhere serene and quiet for my final years.

Instead, we kept hiking uphill, and then running downhill, jogging 14-minute miles, and 17-minute miles, and the only positive thing I could think through the lightning bolts shooting through my feet and legs every step was: It's Mile 75 and I'm still able to run. It's Mile 79 and I'm still running. It's Mile 80, oh wow, they have pancakes at this aid station. It's Mile 81, and I'm still running.

In the summer of 1957, in the kitchen of the house at 4411 Westminster Place in St. Louis, two improvisational theatre performers spent two weeks trying to come up with some solid principles for improv. Elaine May and Ted Flicker were members of The Compass Players, a group founded in 1955 in Chicago by Paul Sills and David Shepherd.

The rules May and Flicker established, as recorded in Janet Colman's 1991 book *The Compass: The Improvisational Theatre that Revolutionized American Comedy*[42], were:

(1) whatever verbal or pantomimed reality that is brought to the stage by one player may not be negated or denied by the other;

(2) while improvising, a player has infinite opportunities for choice, and it is better to take an active than a passive choice; and

(3) in an improvisation, where there are no lines, or given actions, or dramaturgical "spine" to set a character in motion, you are your character, although not one called by your name. All characterization or "acting" comes from an exaggerated or intensified rendition of yourself called by another name.

May and Flicker's principles became known as The Kitchen Rules, and continue to help guide improv performers to the present day. Paul Sills went on to found Chicago's famous improv theater, The Second City, which became a training ground for dozens of comedians, actors, and directors, including Bill Murray, John Belushi, Tina Fey, Amy Poehler, Steve Carell, and Jordan Peele.

The first of The Kitchen Rules, "whatever verbal or pantomimed reality that is brought to the stage by one player may not be negated or denied by the other," became known as "the first rule of improv," and has been paraphrased as "agreeing to the reality that is brought to the stage," and also further shortened to, "Yes, and."

Several decades after its creation, more than a few people started to point out that the first rule of improv applied quite well as a tool for resilience in other areas of life: "Yes, and ..." is accepting reality and working with that reality, instead of "But ...", spending time wishing things were different.

Almost 10 of the final 18 miles of the Hellbender 100 were uphill. The route climbed a dirt road, and then eventually became singletrack. We hiked, hardly talking, as the pain in my feet was now consuming almost all of my brain, save for the part that kept my arms and legs moving. The only thing that seemed to help were the grunts I made with each step, in sync with the shot of pain that fired every time either shoe impacted the ground.

It was not my most glorious athletic moment, and I somehow made it last almost eight hours. I was unable to deal with the pain in any way that would allow me to take big steps, or move quickly. Even when we got to the top of the climb and had just 6.5 miles to go, I had to gingerly pick my way down the singletrack, my breathing tight, the muscles in my face clenched, walking like a 90-year-old with severe arthritis, not an athlete five decades younger with mostly healthy joints and all his cartilage. I cycled through feelings of anger and sadness while trying to find someone to blame, but then reminding myself that I had no one to blame for this but me.

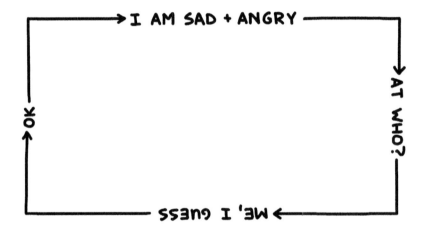

Well, everybody does something, usually anyway. We thought we would do this and it would be fun.

"As far as we can tell, from a purely scientific viewpoint, human life has absolutely no meaning. Humans are the outcome of blind evolutionary processes that operate without goal or purpose. Our actions are not part of some divine cosmic plan, and if planet Earth were to blow up tomorrow morning, the universe would probably keep going about its business as usual. As far as we can tell at this point, human subjectivity would not be missed. Hence any meaning that people ascribe to their lives is just a delusion. The other-worldly meanings medieval people found in their lives were no more deluded than the modern humanist, nationalist and capitalist meanings modern people find. The scientist who says her life is meaningful because she increases the store of human knowledge, the soldier who declares that his life is meaningful because he fights to defend his homeland, and the entrepreneur who finds meaning in building a new company are no less delusional than their medieval counterparts who found meaning in reading scriptures, going on a crusade or building a new cathedral. So perhaps happiness is synchronising one's personal delusions of meaning with the prevailing collective delusions. As long as my personal narrative is in line with the narratives of the people around me, I can convince myself that my life is meaningful, and find happiness in that conviction.

This is quite a depressing conclusion. Does happiness really depend on self-delusion?"

— Yuval Noah Harari, *Sapiens: A Brief History of Humankind*[43]

Kenny and Eve Shopsin opened Shopsin's General Store on a corner in New York's Greenwich Village in 1973, and after a bottle bill was passed in 1983 to encourage recycling, Kenny decided to get rid of soda in cans and bottles and switch to a soda fountain. As a business that sold soda in bottles and cans, under the law, he'd have to accept returns of bottles and cans from anyone—and he didn't want to deal with it. So he got a soda fountain, which eliminated the bottle-return problem, until his landlord hiked up the rent. He had been selling sandwiches out of the store for a while, as well as some takeout-style food throughout the week. To afford the rent, he realized, he'd have to sell a lot more fountain soda. So he and Eve turned Shopsin's General Store into a restaurant, which, at the beginning, had a reasonably-sized menu.

Over the years, the restaurant became a New York institution, almost in spite of Kenny's personality—he hated publicity, and when tourism guidebooks would call the restaurant to confirm details, he would tell the caller that the restaurant had closed. If the restaurant was somehow mentioned in print, Kenny was referred to by writers as "foul-mouthed." In her 2017 memoir, Kenny's daughter, Tamara Shopsin, called him a "militant Buddha." Parties of more than four were not just prohibited; if a party of five showed up and tried to pose as separate parties of three and two, they were kicked out. Every item on the menu was cooked to order in the restaurant's tiny kitchen, and the menu eventually swelled to 900-plus items. Substitutions were not allowed.

Another rent increase came in 2002, and the Shopsins were unable to work it out with the landlord, so they elected to move to a new location. Filmmaker Matt Mahurin decided to document the closing of the restaurant and its ensuing move. Throughout the film, *I Like Killing Flies*, Shopsin intermittently metes out bits of his life philosophy. In one segment in which he doesn't use the F-word at all, Shopsin says:

"The way I choose to function is to pick an arbitrary, stupid goal, become totally involved in it, and pursue it with vigor, and what happens to you in that pursuit is your life."

Studies have shown that when we have children, our happiness decreases, but our sense of meaning and purpose increases[44]. If you're convinced you don't want to have kids, it's hard to understand why anyone would voluntarily decrease their happiness by raising kids. If you're not a Muslim, traveling hundreds, or thousands, of miles to Mecca is not Hajj; it's just a sightseeing trip. If you're not Catholic, the unleavened bread served at mass has no connection to Jesus Christ—it's a cracker. If you don't care about American football, the Super Bowl is just a great day to eat a bunch of food and see the advertising industry's best (or most expensive) work. If you don't particularly have a thing for grass, it's hard to comprehend why people would spend so many hours and resources to maintain a large swath of inedible plants surrounding their house and keep them at a uniform height through the summer.

If you don't believe an ultramarathon will be meaningful to you, it probably just sounds like a really bad idea. Even if you believe it will be meaningful, at some point, you are likely to think it was a really bad idea. But you might still keep going, depending on how invested you are in the meaning you believe you will attain from finishing the race.

Mentally, I was worn out, almost numb, by the time we hit the final descent. The downhill was two and a half miles that took an hour to negotiate. Had someone been shooting video, I would have looked less like a 40-year-old endurance athlete of adequately sound body and mind, more like a blindfolded person relying heavily on trekking poles while trying to navigate down an endless set of icy steps. I scanned the trees for the entire hour, looking for a bit of non-natural color that would signify a tent, or a car, which would signify the end.

Finally, the bright-red finishing arch appeared, just down the hill, in the middle of a grassy meadow. As we got closer, I mumbled to Hilary, "I'm not running," because what was the point of running now, after 36 hours and 10 minutes of dragging ass across the mountains?

We stepped off the singletrack onto the grass for the final few hundred steps to the arch, and I jogged through it, holding Hilary's hand. Aaron, the race director, gave me a hug and handed me a belt buckle with an engraving of an Eastern Hellbender salamander and the words "Hellbender One Hundred Finisher."

I give my congratulations to the winner among your number, and my acknowledgements of valor to the losers.

I sat down in a camp chair 10 feet past the finish line and chatted with Aaron. Someone handed me a pizza box with some cold slices in it. I had finished in 57th place, in 36 hours and 13 minutes. Sixty-nine runners would finish the race before the final 40-hour cutoff, and 11 people didn't finish. A handful of runners came through the finishing arch in the 20 or so minutes after me, and Hilary and I hobbled to the rental car. I fell asleep in the passenger seat shortly after Hilary started driving, dipping in and out of consciousness all the way back to our Airbnb.

I was able to stay upright in the shower, and even wash my feet. We cleaned off the point of one of the safety pins that had held my race bib to my shorts, and I popped my blisters, surprised at how small they were, and that there were only six of them.

I got into the bed to lie down as Hilary—who was, at this point, well on her way to being canonized as a saint in the nondenominational (and, OK, nonexistent) Church of Ultrarunning—cooked some quick food on the stove. I started rubbing my feet together, and in what I can only describe as the most orgasmic non-sexual experience of my life, the pleasure center of my brain lit up and just kept going. If a person's first experience with heroin felt as good as this, I could see why it was so addictive. After a couple minutes, I was too tired to keep going, and I fell asleep. Hilary woke me up a few minutes later to invite me to the kitchen table to eat dinner. According to the Strava app I'd been using to track my movement, I had burned just over 20,000 calories, which would take several meals to even begin to replace.

When I woke up the next morning, I could still move my arms and legs just fine, with a little creaking. With my blisters now popped, walking was no problem. And I had absolutely zero urgency to do anything. We went to a breakfast and lunch joint and I ordered one and a half meals, and then we drove into Asheville to meet friends for dinner later. I stopped at Ben & Jerry's to consume 700 calories of ice cream as an appetizer.

At a book signing in 2016, I met a guy who had been struck by lightning some-where high in the mountains in Colorado. He said he dealt with chronic pain in his feet and elsewhere in his body, but didn't like to take pain medication. So he had, for the past several years, mitigated the pain by doing hard physical activities, in the hopes of a lengthy release of endorphins that would dull his chronic pain for a while afterward. He said that depending on intensity of the activity, the ensuing endorphin release could mask the pain for anywhere from a few days to almost two weeks.

Over the final eight months of the year following the Hellbender, I ran the 100-mile Bighorn Trail Race in Wyoming, the Bear Chase Trail Race 50K near Denver, and the Mines of Spain 100K in Iowa. I also ran the Colfax Marathon in Denver because it started less than a mile from our house, as well as the Missoula Marathon, and the New York City Marathon. I ended up running 52 marathon-length distances that year, because I wanted to do something "interesting" the year I turned 40.

I didn't do that many official marathon races, where I'd have to sign up, pay an entry fee, travel, and run with hundreds or thousands of other people. That seemed like a lot of planning, and probably stress. I would often just take off from the house with my vest full of water and run laps around City Park in Denver until I hit 26.2. Sometimes I would take the dog with me for the first three or four miles, and then drop him off at home before I finished the rest of the marathon.

Ultramarathons counted as two or three marathons. I would start my watch at the beginning of the race, and around 26.2 or 26.3 miles, I'd stop it and restart it.

It was, strangely, less stressful for me to get 40 miles of running in a week by doing runs of 26.2 miles, 8 miles, and 6 miles than it was for me to figure out how to schedule five or six shorter runs that totaled 40 miles. My biggest obstacle with running was often forcing myself to just get out the door, and if I only had to do that three times instead of five, it was easier mentally. I adopted a Mark Twain quote—that was not at all about running—as my mantra: "It is easier to stay out than get out."

Non-scientifically, this is how my addict brain works:

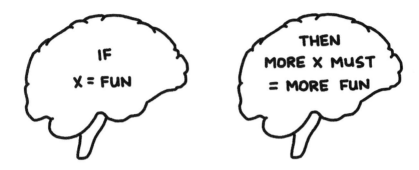

Anyone who's drunk too many beers a few times in their life can tell you this is faulty logic. But it makes sense to an alcoholic, or a crack addict, or someone who's addicted to shopping or porn or gambling, who might put it like this: "Once I start, I can't stop."

Or, as recovering crack addict turned ultramarathoner Charlie Engle told *Men's Journal*'s Adam Higginbotham in 2011: "I am an extremist. My personality, when you take it as a whole...there really is no in-between. My quest has been for balance—but that's a lifelong effort."

One version of heaven, for me, might be a life in which I could do as much as I wanted of whatever I wanted, and it would never decrease in enjoyment. The tenth beer would feel just as good as the first and second one. The seventh cup of coffee would wake me up just like the first sip that morning.

One day in my early 40s, I was finally able to admit to myself that six cups of strong coffee per day was actually not that fun—or at least the fifth and sixth cups weren't. And I dialed it back to four cups. This was a milestone.

My recovering addict brain, on the other hand, has told me for a couple decades now that sobriety is a job, to be completed every day. Black and white, no gray. You either make it through the day without drinking alcohol or you don't. You are not "trying to cut down on my drinking," or "taking it easy on the booze." You do the job, no days off, no fudging your time card, no "just this once." The rules are very simple. This kind of thinking can apply to other things in life, but if you apply it to everything, it's not really sustainable, and people might think you're not so fun to be around.

Forest and I ran most of the last 20-mile loop of the 2019 Mines of Spain 100K in the dark, hiking the bigger climbs and running everything else on the rolling hills along the Mississippi River in Dubuque, Iowa. My legs were tired, I was tired, and when we hit the final few hundred feet to the finish line, I was ready to be done. We completed 62 miles in just under 14 hours. We shook hands with Josh, the race director, got our finisher medals, and went back to our Airbnb to eat pizza. We'd had a full day, running almost two and a half marathons, and I still got to bed before midnight. No slogging through the night, no sleep deprivation, no watching the sun come up and realizing I still had 20 or 30 miles left to go. It was nice.

There's a saying, "All things in moderation," which makes sense to people who can eat a little bit of dessert, or drink one and a half beers, or pull the handle of a slot machine a couple times and walk away if it doesn't hit.

I had long preferred the version that goes, "All things in moderation, including moderation." And 62 miles felt pretty moderate, relatively, anyway.

I got hired to speak at a corporate retreat a month after I finished my 52 marathons. After the presentation, a woman came up to chat with me. She said she'd never run a marathon and had been discouraged by her husband's comments. She had mentioned to him that a friend of hers had finished a marathon recently, and he had asked what her time was. When she told him her friend's marathon time, he said, "That's not very fast." I asked her: Has he run a marathon?

"Oh, no way," she said.

Mark Twain did, once, technically complete an ultramarathon[45]. In November 1874, Twain left Hartford, Connecticut, with his pastor, J.H. Twitchell, in hopes of making it to Boston in two days. The two had enjoyed many 10-mile walks together, and in the late 1860s, the idea of walking 100 miles all at once had become a bit of a craze in America, with many men and women trying to cover the arbitrary distance, and often succeeding.

Twain and Twitchell made it 28 miles into their attempt on the first day before deciding that it had become not very fun and "was actually hard work." They stopped and slept, and in the morning, walked seven more miles to a train station and took the train into Boston.

In October 2019, the running world's attention turned to the INEOS 1:59 Challenge, humankind's best, and most expensive, attempt at seeing if the marathon distance of 26.2 miles could be run in under two hours. Kenyan runner and world marathon record holder Eliud Kipchoge would run in Nike shoes with a carbon plate sandwiched between high-tech foam in the midsole, on a sea-level course mapped for its flatness and straightness, and be preceded by a rotating team of pacers who would run in formation to block any wind, behind a pace car showing their per-mile pace and a laser marking the fastest route on the road. In all, 43 of the world's fastest runners ran with Kipchoge, seven people at a time. From overhead, the group of runners looked like this:

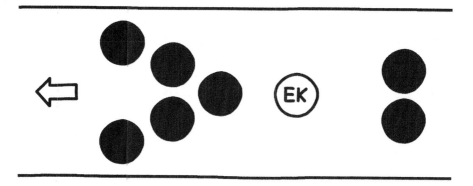

In the end, Kipchoge broke the 2-hour mark, with a time of 1:59:40, in an exhibition "so heavily engineered that his new time will not count as a world record," as Paul Bisceglio, wrote in *The Atlantic*. To those who were excited about it, it was a watershed moment: A human being had finally run, in under two hours, the 26.2-mile distance that had so captured our imagination since Pheidippides' legendary journey from Marathon to Athens in 490 BC. Would you, though, have a hard time explaining to, say, a four-year-old why it was a such a big deal, involving so many people, so much planning, and so many resources? Sure.

It turns out that Pheidippides' run from Marathon to Athens, the story that forms the basis of our marathon racing tradition, wasn't exactly 26.2 miles or 42.195 kilometers. It's generally believed that his run was around 25 miles, or 40 kilometers, which was the length of the first modern marathon race at the 1896 Athens Olympic Games. And the first few non-Olympic marathon races that followed, as well as the 1900 and 1904 Olympic Games. [46]

But at the London Olympics in 1908, the marathon race was planned to start at Windsor Castle and finish in the new White City Stadium in West London, where the Queen would be watching from a box at the finish line. That distance was 26 miles, but then the queen wanted the royal children to be able to watch the start of the race from their nursery, so the start was moved back 385 yards to the East Lawn of the castle. Which made the 1908 Olympic Marathon 26.2 miles, or 42.195 kilometers. The 26.2-mile distance was adopted as the standard marathon distance by the International Amateur Athletic Federation in 1921, and became the official Olympic marathon distance in 1924.

Another part of the Pheidippides marathon story: Before the 25-mile run from Marathon to Athens, as the Persians were about to land at Marathon, he was actually sent from Athens to Sparta to request troops to fight the invading Persians. As the story goes, he covered the distance of about 150 miles in two days. For religious reasons, the Spartans could not join the Athenian army to fight for six more days, so Pheidippides had to hustle back to Athens to deliver the news. So back to Athens he ran, in about two days. [47]

What I'm saying is that before Pheidippides ran the first marathon, the legendary story upon which we have built our marathon tradition, he ran the first ultramarathon. Or the first two ultramarathons, depending on how you view his rest break in between his two 150-mile runs.

But the marathon story grabbed our attention first and became foremost, somehow. Despite being a much less epic feat, it was more meaningful to us. Why? Ultrarunner and author Dean Karnazes has a theory why, as he wrote in his 2016 book *The Road to Sparta* (excerpted in *Runner's World*): "Perhaps because in that final jaunt from the battlefield of Marathon to Athens, the mystic messenger supposedly died at the conclusion. To the ancient Greeks, nothing could be nobler than dying after performing a heroic deed for one's country."

IV.

When a pandemic spread across the globe in 2020, everything paused, including races. We moved to Montana, convinced that we'd probably never be able to afford a space bigger than 850 square feet in Denver. In our new hometown, the closest trails were two miles from our front door, as opposed to 20 miles of freeway driving.

At the beginning of the year, I got a cold that turned into a chronic cough, and while I visited doctors and tried to figure it out, I took a break from running. Once it was clear that running wasn't exacerbating it, I started up again from zero. By the time we moved at the beginning of July, I was back up to 25 or 30 miles a week, but had only run 420 miles the entire year.

I had no goals for the year, aside from not contracting the plague. I was not bummed out that there were no ultramarathons, especially with dozens of new trails to explore nearby.

By early fall, some races had returned, with adjusted formats—fewer entrants, spreading out runners with staggered start times. But I wasn't missing races enough to enter one, or travel. I figured I'd just wait for races to go back to normal, and then I'd start going again.

My forays into the mountains near town had gradually grown since my first 10-mile run to the top of Mt. Sentinel our first week: miles, then 13 miles, then 15, then 18.7 miles climbing 4,200 vertical feet to the top of Stuart Peak and back. At the end of August, I put together a 30-mile loop and decided to bike the eight miles to the trailhead. I got a late start, became dehydrated, and then realized I had miscalculated by about five miles, and it was actually 35 miles, not 30 miles. When I got a cell signal with about four miles to go, I texted Hilary to let her know I was OK but was running late. She offered to come pick me up at the trailhead, sparing me the bike ride home in the dark, and I accepted, only semi-reluctantly.

In the evenings all summer and fall, I had been poking around a mapping website, drawing a line connecting a bunch of trails in the Rattlesnake Creek drainage, trying to build a 50-plus-mile loop that would start and end at a trailhead. After a few hours over the course of several weeks, I had drawn up a plan that summited five peaks, over 60-ish miles of running and hiking, and about 12,000 feet of elevation gain. I could get water from a couple alpine lakes and creeks along the way, except for the last 30 miles, which would almost certainly be dry. So I planned to pack a bear-proof canister with a four-liter water reservoir and some food, and drive it up a dirt road to a trailhead, where I'd hide it a little ways off my planned route and be able to resupply the day of my big run.

It was a bad plan. The afternoon before I had scheduled my big run, I packed the bear canister and drove to the dirt road that would lead to the trailhead where I'd leave the food and water cache. A locked gate was closed near the bottom of the road, which meant if I wanted to cache my food and water, I'd have to hike it in several miles and 3,000-plus vertical feet, and then back, which is not something I wanted to be doing the day before I attempted a 60-mile day in the mountains.

So I drove home, deciding I'd just figure out a different way to do it.

I parked my car at the Cherry Street trailhead, carrying a 72-ounce hydration reservoir in my vest, as well as two water bottles, including my squeeze filter. I had a Garmin InReach in my vest so Hilary could track me, and so I could send an SOS signal in case of emergency. I also chose to carry a can of bear spray, which would hopefully prevent one type of emergency that might necessitate sending an SOS signal. The downside was it weighed a pound and took up valuable space in my vest that I could have otherwise used to carry another 20 ounces of water. It was 43 degrees and sunny, and I hopped out of the car wearing running shorts, a T-shirt, and a light hooded wind jacket. I locked the car, clipped the key inside my vest, and took off jogging through the neighborhood to the first trailhead at 8:10 a.m., trying to minimize the bouncing of the nearly seven pounds of water sloshing around in my vest.

If you surveyed the people who run ultramarathons about why they spend their time running ridiculously long distances on trails, you'd probably get several different answers, from just enjoying being a part of the running community to loving competition.

As I hiked up Water Works Hill above town, making progress on my first mile out of 60 miles, and my first few hundred feet of climbing out of 12,000 feet, it had now been five years since I'd run my first 50K. If this lark I was on had a story back then, it might have been: I was curious if I could run an ultramarathon. As I moved up through the distances, I could have said: I knew people ran 100 miles all in one go, and I wanted to see if I could too.

If I wanted to prove to myself that I could do those things, I already had. I wasn't fast, but I made it to the finish line every time. So if that was done, I needed another story to tell myself, in order to get through 60 miles on my own, with my vest full of snacks and bear spray.

"In 2009, neurophysiologist Johanna Meijer set up an unusual experiment in her backyard. In an ivy-tangled corner of her garden, she and her colleagues at Leiden University in the Netherlands placed a rodent running wheel inside an open cage and trained a motion-detecting infrared camera on the scene. Then they put out a dish of food pellets and chocolate crumbs to attract animals to the wheel and waited.

Wild house mice discovered the food in short order, then scampered into the wheel and started to run. Rats, shrews, and even frogs found their way to the wheel—more than 12,000 animals over 3 years. The creatures seemed to relish the feeling of running without going anywhere.

The study 'puts a nail in the coffin' of the debate over whether mice and rats will run on wheels in a natural setting, says Ted Garland, an evolutionary physiologist at the University of California, Riverside, who was not involved in the work. More importantly, he says, the findings suggest that like (some) humans, mice and other animals may simply exercise because they like to."

—Emily Underwood, "Even in the Wild, Mice Run on Wheels," Science.org[48]

At this point, I had turned in a manuscript that would become a book with the half-joking title *I Hate Running and You Can Too*. I had a pretty strong argument for hating running: It didn't feel enjoyable until I was 45 or 50 minutes into a run, when (I assumed) my body began producing endorphins. I would procrastinate my runs until late in the day, after I'd had a chance to drink coffee, eat breakfast, then lunch, do a bunch of work and maybe some associated errands, and then I'd even get dressed to run, and continue to procrastinate my run for several minutes or hours, while wearing running clothes—which is not ideal apparel for, say, cutting wood in your garage for a minor carpentry project that obviously couldn't wait until you got home from your run, you fucking dipshit.

But I kept doing these long runs of 10 miles, 15 miles, 20 miles. My running vest had become sort of a security blanket, or a charm I carried on my shoulders that brought not good luck, but the guarantee of a worthwhile experience. With my vest on, I could get to a place far enough from the trailhead where I was more likely to run into a deer or elk than a human, or at least have enough solitude to clear my head for a few minutes at a time. I felt good the day after, when I could notice the slightest twinges of pain in a few joints, or muscle soreness that indicated that I'd done a lot of climbing, or run down a steeper trail than usual. On days that I didn't have that pain present, I began to feel an itchy need to get back out there.

The short runs were maintenance: washing dishes, shopping for ingredients, wiping down the stove. The long runs were when I got to cook the meals, have fun, and mess up the kitchen a little bit. I got to enjoy the food I cooked. And it didn't matter if I was running with a few hundred people or totally alone, or if I ran fast because I felt light, or ran slow as molasses and hiked all the uphills because I had a stressful week at work. I just needed a few hours to go fuck around in the woods, on my rodent running wheel.

"In the 1970s Richard Solomon of the University of Pennsylvania had shown that the body learns to adjust to all sorts of stimuli. We may get hooked on recreational drugs because they right away make us feel so good, but activities like sauna bathing, marathon running, or parachute jumping, which initially cause discomfort and even terror, can ultimately become very enjoyable. This gradual adjustment signals that a new chemical balance has been established within the body, so that marathon runners, say, get a sense of well-being and exhilaration from pushing their bodies to the limit.

At this point, just as with drug addiction, we start to crave the activity and experience withdrawal when it's not available. In the long run people become more preoccupied with the pain of withdrawal than the activity itself. This theory could explain why some people hire someone to beat them, or burn themselves with cigarettes, or why they are only attracted to people who hurt them. Fear and aversion, in some perverse way, can be transformed into pleasure."

—Bessel van der Kolk, M.D., *The Body Keeps the Score: Brain, Mind, and Body in the Healing of Trauma*[49]

Despite all the mileage I was doing, I still felt like the king of procrastinating running until the last minute. I never did it first thing in the morning, even during the hot summer months, and most days, I'd find a way to put it off until way late in the afternoon, in the spring and fall sometimes finishing my last few miles in the dark.

Every time, I felt so good after my run. Any mild anxiety, the frantic feeling I'd have throughout every day that I wasn't getting enough done, or that I should be more efficient, had melted away. And almost every time, I would think to myself, "I should start running earlier in the day, so I can feel good for a bigger chunk of my day instead of just the last few hours before I go to bed." But of course I wouldn't.

But by the time I got out the door, I figured I might as well make the most of my inertia and keep running as far as I could. If I could get out and go, I might as well go long.

In her 2019 book, *The Joy of Movement*[50], psychologist Kelly McGonigal writes about studies of endocannabinoids, the brain chemicals that are mimicked by marijuana, and that happen to be released by certain types of exercise:

"... many of the effects of cannabis are consistent with descriptions of exercise-induced highs, including the sudden disappearance of worries or stress, a reduction in pain, the slowing of time, and a heightening of the senses."

McGonigal cites the work of University of Arizona anthropologist David Raichlen, who wanted to document the actual release of endocannabinoids during exercise. He had subjects get on a treadmill for 30 minutes, and he found that runners who jogged on a treadmill tripled their levels of endocannabinoids, but people who walked on a treadmill or ran at maximum effort for the same amount of time got no effect.

I trucked up the trail through a pine forest, the bushes lining the singletrack starting to turn red and gold as fall drew closer. I was moving fast, every once in a while reminding myself out loud to keep an all-day pace. The route I had drawn on the map would take me to the summits of Stuart Peak (7,791 ft), Mosquito Peak (8,057 feet), Mineral Peak (7,447 feet), Sheep Mountain (7,646 feet), and Mt. Jumbo (4,546 feet), with a couple of big sustained climbs. The elevation profile looked like this:

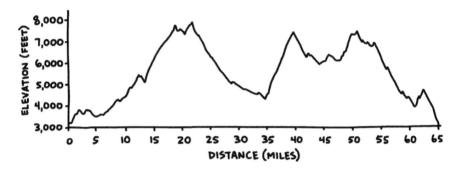

I had told Hilary I thought I'd be finished with the whole loop by, I don't know, maybe 10 or 11 p.m.? Midnight at the latest, I said. She didn't laugh at me.

"The pride and tradition of the Montana Grizzlies will not be entrusted to the timid or the weak."

—University of Montana football sign on the south side of Washington-Grizzly Stadium, facing the M Trailhead on Mt. Sentinel, 2021-2022

"Let me tell you: We are here on Earth to fart around, and don't let anybody ever tell you any different."

—Kurt Vonnegut, speaking at Case Western Reserve University[51], February 4, 2004

I summited Stuart Peak around Mile 19, after almost five hours of continuously moving. Was it going more slowly than I thought it would? Maybe a little. I bushwhacked over to the summit of Mosquito Peak, and found the trail again and started the descent to the alpine lakes below. The lakes are in designated wilderness, so the only way to access them is by foot, and from any direction, that requires a minimum of 10 miles of walking or running. So the trails to them are narrow, rocky, tight, and don't see a ton of human traffic, or maintenance. It's a great place to hear nothing besides your own breath as you run downhill.

You might also hear a grouse exploding out of the underbrush, two feet off the side of the trail, when you're three steps away from it, with a boom and then a flap of wings. Then you draw in all your breath in a huge gasp, nearly fall over, and catch yourself just in time before you tumble into a tree. And then you realize it was not a gunshot or a land mine, just a bird the size of a soccer ball.

Kelly McGonigal titled the second chapter of *The Joy of Movement* "Getting Hooked," and the thesis of the chapter is that humans can become dependent on exercise, for all the benefits it provides. Makes sense, I thought, as I read it. And then, McGonigal writes:

In a laboratory experiment at the University of Wisconsin, Madison, researchers set out to capture what happens in the brains of mice who love wheel-running but are denied the opportunity. Just before their nightly run, the researchers blocked each mouse's access to the running wheel. The mice were ready to exercise but couldn't—as if you had shown up at the gym excited to work out, only to find the doors locked and the lights off. In that moment of thwarted desire, each mouse was sacrificed. The researchers scooped out its brain, slicing and staining the gray matter for examination. Under a microscope, they observed chemical evidence that the mouse had been in a state of heightened longing when it died. Areas of the brain associated with desire, motivation, frustration, and even the physical initiation of running were coactivated[52].

Lab mice do not usually die of natural causes. Most mice do not live lives worthy of Beverly Cleary books or Disney movies. They're mice, and they like to run. Or they often learn to like to run.

If you're objective about it, it's an interesting study, showing that mice can become addicted to exercise just like they could substances such as nicotine, heroin, or sugar. Rationally, as a human, you might know that we study lab rats and mice to discover things about humans, because rats and mice are similar to us genetically, physiologically, and anatomically. So your takeaway might be that if mice can get addicted to exercise, so can humans.

But reading that study, I just felt bad for the mice. They just wanted to run, like I do, after a long day of sitting around. And just when they got excited and thought they were going to get to take off and rip around the wheel for a while, which was probably the highlight of their day, somebody killed them.

I stopped to filter water at Little Lake, a light breeze buffing the surface of the lake into hundreds of sparkling peaks, the dark cliffs of the north face of Mosquito Peak dropping a thousand feet into its south end. I hustled off and ran down the singletrack through the trees, and then the fire road as it dropped toward Rattlesnake Creek. With one last big view before I dipped into the trees again, I looked south and considered that the sun might be a little lower than I'd have liked it to be at this point in my run. It was taking longer than I'd estimated. I may have not exactly told Hilary the truth about what time I'd get home—not because I was lying, but because I was basing my estimate on optimism instead of actual data. Time, unfortunately, doesn't expand or contract according to your attitude—it's math.

When I've been moving on my own feet for 25 or 30 miles, with many more miles to go, I feel many things: fatigue, minor aches and pains that shift from one body part to the next, hot spots from friction inside my shoes, a slight burning in my lungs and throat, maybe a bit of self-pity or self-loathing that I have to keep going for several more hours and I have no one to blame for it but myself, all the stuff that happens when you push a mostly desk-sitting body to travel dozens of miles under its own power, something you can do because you have the time and resources and life situation that enables a foolish pursuit like running around in the woods for an entire day.

If I run that list through my head and get to the end of it, sometimes I feel what I should be feeling: lucky. Like a lab rat getting a few hours to romp around in Rat Park.

At Mile 35, I came to a trail junction. It was 5:00 p.m., and it would be dark at 7:00 p.m. My legs were hammered. I had made a plan for 2019 me, and 2020 me hadn't trained quite as much. My last water source was either behind me, or maybe a mile ahead of me on the trail, and after that, probably nothing.

If I turned right at the trail junction, I could bail on the whole idea: I'd be able to casually jog and walk the mostly flat eight miles of fire road and trail to the main Rattlesnake Trailhead, where I could call Hilary and ask if she'd come pick me up. Or maybe I'd just get an Uber. It was a path to more immediate happiness, comfort, the big red EASY button from those office supply store commercials.

If I turned left, I had at least 25 miles to go, maybe more (I was starting to think my mapping estimate was a little bit off). Two hours of daylight, the next five miles straight up a 3,000-foot climb, and after that, more ups and downs. Maybe I could get reception from the top of one of the next couple of peaks and at least text Hilary that I'd be a couple hours late. The amount of fun I was having per hour was definitely trending downward, and an upward spike was not likely if I continued left, up, and onward into the dark.

No one was making me do this. It was just an idea, a line I'd drawn on a map. I made the whole thing up. Like so many other stories we dream up, I was in the middle of the third act of a three-act narrative. Or, less dramatically: my latest arbitrary, stupid goal.

I twisted the bite valve of my hydration reservoir, looking up the trail to the left, then to the easy exit to the right.

Well, everybody does something, usually, anyway.

<u>**Notes**</u>

1. Western States Endurance Run, "The Golden Minute — Western States 100," Facebook, 2015, https://www.facebook.com/watch/?v=101533071 28530412

2. Bryon Powell, *Relentless Forward Progress: A Guide to Running Ultramarathons* (Breakaway Books, 2011), 106.

3. Kelly Lambert, *The Lab Rat Chronicles: A Neuroscientist Reveals Life Lessons from the Planet's Most Successful Mammals* (TarcherPerigee, 2011), 74-78.

4. Steven J. Dubner, "A Better Way to Eat," Freakonomics, July 3, 2014. https://freakonomics.com/podcast/a-better-way-to-eat/

5. Nir Eyal, "How to Achieve Your Goals By Creating an Enemy" https://www.nirandfar.com/goals-enemy/

6. Brad Kim, "Pizza Rat," September 22, 2015. https://knowyourmeme.com/memes/pizza-rat

7. Nicolás Medina Mora, "We Spoke To The Guy Who Filmed The Pizza Rat Video," BuzzFeed, September 21, 2015. https://www.buzzfeednews.com/article/nicolasmedinamora/meet-the-pizza-rat-videographer

8. Lisa Respers France, "Pizza Rat: Our newest obsession," CNN.com, September 24, 2015. https://www.cnn.com/2015/09/22/living/pizza-rat-feat/index.html

9. Dean Karnazes, *Ultramarathon Man: Confessions of an All-Night Runner* (TarcherPerigee, 2006), 11.

10. David Ertl, "RAGBRAI Training: Think Iowa's Flat? Think Again." Ragbrai.com, February 20, 2011. https://ragbrai.com/ragbrai-training-think-iowas-flat-think-again/

11. Robert B. Cialdini, Richard J. Borden, Avril Thorne, Marcus Randall Walker, Stephen Freeman, and Lloyd Reynolds Sloan, "Basking in Reflected Glory: Three (Football) Field Studies," Journal of Personality and Social Psychology, Vol. 34, No. 3, (1976): 366-375.

12. Cindy Boren, "James Harrison thinks kids' participation trophies are worthless, sets off debate," Washington Post, August 16, 2015. https://www.washingtonpost.com/news/early-lead/wp/2015/08/1 6/james-harrison-wont-let-his-kids-get-participation-trophies/

13. Charles Curtis, "Cardinals coach goes off on participation trophies," USA Today, December 3, 2016. https://www.usatoday.com/story/sports/ftw/2016/12/03/louisville-wom ens-hoops-coach-goes-off-on-participation-trophies-in-fiery-postgame-rant /94901590/

14. Davy Crockett, "Ultrarunning's Endurance Ride Roots," Ultrarunning History, May 22, 2018. https://ultrarunninghistory.com/ultrarunnings-e ndurance-ride-roots/, http://www.crockettclan.org/ultras/endurance-rid e-roots.pdf

15. Devin Kelly, "Children in the Garden: On Life at a 3,100-Mile Race," Longreads, January 6, 2022. https://longreads.com/2022/01/06/children -in-the-garden-devin-kelly/

16. Robin A. Smith, "Is There a Limit to Human Endurance? Science Says Yes," Duke Today, June 5, 2019, https://today.duke.edu/2019/06/there-limit-h uman-endurance-science-says-yes

17. Caitlin Thurber, Lara R. Dugas, Cara Ocobock, Bryce Carlson, John R. Speakman, and Herman Pontzer, "Extreme events reveal an alimentary limit on sustained maximal human energy expenditure," Science Advances, Vol. 5 Issue 6 (June 2019): https://www.science.org/doi/10.1126/sciadv.aaw0341

18. Lulu Garcia-Navarro, "The Limits Of Human Endurance," Weekend Edition, NPR, June 9, 2019. https://www.npr.org/2019/06/09/731044430/ the-limits-of-human-endurance

19. Scottie Andrew and Saeed Ahmed, "The two groups that reach the peak of human endurance? Extreme athletes and pregnant women," CNN.com, June 6, 2019. https://www.cnn.com/2019/06/06/health/pregnant-wome n-peak-endurance-trnd/index.html

20. M. Khodaee, J. Spittler, P. Basset, K. Vanbaak, J.C. Hill, I. San Millán, and M.D. Hoffman. "Reasons for Inability to Complete Ultramarathons: A Multicenter Study," British Journal of Sports Medicine (2014) 48: 618-619 https://bjsm.bmj.com/content/48/7/618.3

21. Sonia Cavigelli. "Fear of Novelty in Infant Rats Predicts Adult Corticosterone Dynamics and an Early Death." Proceedings of the National Academy of Sciences, 2003. https://www.academia.edu/13994455/Fear_of_novelty_in_infant _rats_predicts_adult_corticosterone_dynamics_and_an_early_death

22. Paul Ronto and Vania Nikolova, "The State of Ultra Running 2020," Ru nRepeat.com, November 8, 2023. https://runrepeat.com/state-of-ultra-r unning

23. Dan McQuade, "How Far Did Rocky Go in His Training Run in Rocky II?," Philadelphia, September 18, 2013. https://www.phillymag.com/new s/2013/09/18/rocky-training-run-rocky-ii/

24. Mary Hui, "'Not Just a Maid': The Ultra-Running Domestic Workers of Hong Kong," The New York Times, May 25, 2019. https://www.nytime s.com/2019/05/25/world/asia/hong-kong-maids-running.html

25. Doug Mayer, "Ultrarunning Hallucinations Happen. Here's How to Deal With Them," Trail Runner Magazine, January 25, 2017. https://www.tra ilrunnermag.com/training/trail-tips-training/ultrarunning-hallucinations

26. Stephen King: The Long Walk: The Route, https://patcoston.com/steph enking/TheLongWalk-Route.aspx

27. Jim Burnett, "This Third Time Was Anything But Charming – SPOT Misuse At Grand Canyon National Park," National Parks Traveler, October 21, 2009. https://www.nationalparktraveler.org/2009/10/third-time-was-anything -charming-%E2%80%93-spot-misuse-grand-canyon-national-park4790

28. Vodka: The Spirit of the Industry, Distilled Spirits Council of the United States. https://www.distilledspirits.org/wp-content/uploads/2020/04/ Vodka-2019.pdf

29. Jeffrey Steingarten, The Man Who Ate Everything (Vintage, 1998) 7.

30. William Goldman, *Which Lie Did I Tell? More Adventures in the Screen Trade* (Vintage Books, 2000), 256.

31. Charlie Todd, "The Shared Experience of Absurdity," filmed May 2011 at TEDxBloomington, Bloomington, IN, video, 10:01, https://www.ted.co m/talks/charlie_todd_the_shared_experience_of_absurdity

32. John Gonzalez, "The Unexplainable, Undeniably Entertaining Rituals of the Bills Mafia," The Ringer, September 26, 2019. https://www.theringer .com/nfl/2019/9/26/20884655/buffalo-bills-mafia-tailgate

33. Paul Rozin and Keith Kennel. "Acquired preferences for piquant foods by chimpanzees," Appetite, Volume 4, Issue 2 (June 1983): 69-77. https://do i.org/10.1016/S0195-6663(83)80003-8

34. Sarah Berry, "Paul Rozin reveals the link between pleasure and pain, and why some like it hot," The Sydney Morning Herald, January 19, 2015. https://www.smh.com.au/lifestyle/health-and-wellness/paul-rozin-reveals -the-link-between-pleasure-and-pain-and-why-some-like-it-hot-20150119 -12t9oy.html

35. Paul Rozin, Lily Guillot, Katrina Fincher, Alexander Rozin, and Eli Tsukayama, "Glad to be sad, and other examples of benign masochism," Judgment and Decision Making, Volume 8, Issue 4 (July 2013): 439-447

36. Thomas M. Brinthaupt and Richard P. Lipka, *Changing the Self: Philosophies, Techniques, and Experiences* (State University of New York Press, 1994), 161.

37. James Danckert and John D. Eastwood, *Out of My Skull: The Psychology of Boredom* (Harvard University Press, 2020), 22.

38. Bill Donahue, "Fixing Diane's Brain," Runner's World, June 22, 2018. https://www.runnersworld.com/runners-stories/a21763474/fixing -dianes-brain/

39. Mark Phillips, Latif Nasser, Lulu Miller, Jad Abumrad, and Robert Krulwich, "In the Running," Radiolab, April 5, 2011. https://radiolab.org/po dcast/122291-in-running/transcript

40. Susan Cain, *Quiet: The Power of Introverts in a World That Can't Stop Talking* (Crown, 2012), 21.

41. Hugo Münsterberg, *Psychology and Industrial Efficiency* (University Press Cambridge, 1913), 196-198

42. Janet Colman, *The Compass: The Improvisational Theatre that Revolutionized American Comedy* (Centennial Publications of the University of Chicago Press, 1991) 225-226.

43. Yuval Noah Harari, *Sapiens: A Brief History of Humankind* (Harper, 2015), 332.

44. Ana Swanson, "Many parents will say kids made them happier. They're probably lying." The Washington Post, July 6, 2016. https://www.washingtonpost.com/news/wonk/wp/2016/07/06/many-americans-will-tell-you-having-kids-made-them-happier-theyre-probably-lying/

45. Davy Crockett, "55: The 100-miler — Part 2 (1874-1878) Women Pedestrians," Ultrarunning History, May 29, 2020. https://ultrarunninghistory.com/100-miler-part-2/

46. Hugh Jones, *The Expert's Guide to Marathon Training* (Carlton Books, 2004), 8-17.

47. Dean Karnazes, "The Real Pheidippides Story," Runner's World, December 6, 2016. https://www.runnersworld.com/runners-stories/a20836761/the-real-pheidippides-story/

48. Emily Underwood, "Even in the Wild, Mice Run on Wheels," Science.org, May 20, 2014. https://www.science.org/content/article/even-wild-mice-run-wheels

49. Bessel A. Van der Kolk, *The Body Keeps the Score: Brain, Mind, and Body in the Healing of Trauma* (United Kingdom: Penguin Publishing Group, 2015), 32.

50. Kelly McGonigal, *The Joy of Movement: How Exercise Helps Us Find Happiness, Hope, Connection, and Courage* (Penguin Publishing Group, 2019), 16.

51. Kurt Vonnegut, "Kurt Vonnegut Lecture," filmed February 4 2004 at Case Western Reserve University, video, 35:01, https://www.youtube.com/watch?v=4_RUgnC1lm8

52. Kelly McGonigal, *The Joy of Movement: How Exercise Helps Us Find Happiness, Hope, Connection, and Courage* (Penguin Publishing Group, 2019), 63.

Acknowledgements

Thanks to Hilary Oliver, who makes everything in my life better, including this book.

Thanks to Kevin Breen, whose editorial guidance was indispensable.

Thanks to everyone who shared some miles with me during the creation of this book, which happened as much while I was running as while I was sitting at my desk typing the words and drawing the illustrations.

About the author

Brendan Leonard is a columnist at *Outside*, and has written 12 books, including *I Hate Running and You Can Too, Sixty Meters to Anywhere*, and *Make It: 50 Myths and Truths About Creating*. His writing and illustrations have appeared in *National Geographic Adventure, Runner's World, Trail Runner, Alpinist, Red Bulletin*, on CNN.com, and in dozens of other publications. His short films have won several awards and have been screened in 20+ countries around the world. He has completed dozens of ultramarathons, marathons, and other adventures. Find more of his work at Semi-Rad.com and on social media @semi_rad.

Printed in Great Britain
by Amazon

44487022R00172